TEACHING THE SCRIPTURES

**CHRIST JESUS
based on the image on the
Great Chalice of Antioch**

TEACHING THE SCRIPTURES

A Study Guide

for

Bible Students and Teachers

by

Russell D. Robinson, Ph.D.
Professor of Education
University of Wisconsin-Milwaukee

BIBLE STUDY PRESS
9017 N. 70th Street
Milwaukee, Wisconsin 53223-2113
Telephone: (414) 354-3504

ISBN 1-877837-11-3

Printed in the United States of America

To my family

acknowledgments

Any book, no matter how modest, owes its production to many persons, and any list of acknowledgments is always, as a result, incomplete. However, honesty requires the acknowledgment of the support, encouragement, and help of at least a few:

My wife, Helen, who helped in so many ways with the sixth edition including typesetting the entire book and offering many constructive suggestions.

My students whose ideas and suggestions found their way into this considerable revision of the text and the addition of sample "worksheets" for self or group study.

My mother and grandmother who early taught me respect and love for the Bible. Also Will B. Davis and Eunice M. Bayless who inspired me to deeper study of the Bible and Wynona Ashton who encouraged me greatly in carrying through the initial project.

My children who helped in their own ways more than twenty-five years ago during my many hours of work in preparation of the first manuscript over a period of two years and who helped in subsequent years in the distribution of the book.

Students in my adult Bible classes at whose urging the book was first made available and whose use of the book for their own continued study has served the purpose of its writing. Also Sunday School pupils and adult students in my classes over the last 30 years whose questions led me to seek further.

My own teachers in Bible and history of religion courses at the University of Wisconsin, Madison, and elsewhere and my unseen teachers whose writings listed in the bibliography have continued to teach appreciation and understanding of the Scriptures.

I would also like to express appreciation for the thousands whose enthusiastic reception of the first and subsequent printings has made possible this new and expanded sixth edition.

Finally, I am indebted to the Schumakers and Omnibook Company for their craftsmanship and dedication to quality printing.

NOTE

A note about the references is in order. For example, on page 9, the reference given as (Gen. 1:1--2:3) includes all the verses starting with the first verse of chapter one and continuing through the third verse of chapter two, as indicated by the double hyphen. The reference given as (1:1-5) includes verses one through five of chapter one of Genesis, as shown by the hyphen. The name of the book is not repeated for each reference.

On page 17, for example, the reference given as (Gen. 11:31) includes only the thirty-first verse of chapter eleven of Genesis. The next reference (12:1-8) includes verses one through eight of chapter twelve, also in Genesis. The reference given as (Gen. 14) includes all of chapter fourteen.

On page 21, the reference given as (Ex.1--4) includes all of chapters one through four of Exodus. The reference given as (23:20--24:8) includes all the verses from verse twenty of chapter twenty-three through verse eight of chapter twenty-four of Exodus, though the name of the book is not repeated. This system of references is followed throughout this book.

This study guide was prepared initially as notes for a series of Bible lectures I developed more than twenty-five years ago. At the urging of students and friends, it was expanded and made available in book form for those who wished a concise outline for Scriptural study. The book was not intended to be exhaustive or interpretive, though some interpretation is inevitable in a work of this kind. The dates and chronology relating to Bible events or authorship of books are tentative, but represent those on which at least some scholars agree. I have tried to indicate points of differing scholarly judgment where it was deemed requisite. Information has been included on the early Christian Church, material not usually well-known, and the subsequent development of Christianity is traced to our own day.

As with the first edition in 1966, this considerably expanded and thoroughly revised sixth edition is designed to direct the user to the Bible itself. The study of the Scriptures is a challenging and rewarding task. It is hoped that this revised guide will be an even more useful help for Sunday School teachers and others in their own study, as well as in orderly teaching of the Scriptures. Space is provided on each page for students to write in their own notes, comments, and references. The appendix includes helps for Sunday School teachers in developing teaching plans and improving teaching techniques. A selected list of source books and references is included and an extensive list of Bible study aids. Samples of study worksheets are also included for self-study or for group work.

As a general rule, Sunday School children, ages two through seven, may be taught with the Bible story approach, meeting "friends" in the Scriptures, and learning the meaning of helpful Scriptural passages such as the Commandments, Beatitudes, Golden Rule, Lord's Prayer, some of the Psalms, etc. Children, ages eight through thirteen, are ready to learn something of the Bible as a whole, its history, continuity and the relationship and messages of its great characters, focusing first on the life and works of Christ Jesus, then reaching back into the Old Testament and forward into the remainder of the New Testament and Christian history. Young people, ages fourteen through nineteen, and adults upon having attained background in the Bible as a whole, are prepared to concentrate on the great life-themes developed and elaborated throughout the Scriptures, such themes as Life, Love, Truth, sacrament, atonement, immortality, prayer, etc., as well as in-depth study of various books of the Bible.

This study guide is designed to provide important background on the books, authors, messages, characters, stories, chronology, and continuity of the Scriptures. It is well to remember, however, that it is the spiritual import of the Bible that is most important. This is discovered by each individual through prayer, study, spiritual research, and personal experience.

Milwaukee, Wisconsin
January, 1993

contents

OUTLINE OF BOOK

contents

maps and illustrations

Illustrations are from the "Popular and Critical Bible Encyclopedia" (1904) except that on page 68 which is from "Journeys of Jesus" (1883) and that on page 7 which is from "Bible Readings for the Home Circle" (1888), and that on page 57 which is from the third edition of "Science and Health with Key to the Scriptures" (1881). The frontispiece is based on the representation of Jesus on the Great Chalice of Antioch, one of the earliest attempts to portray Jesus, and was drawn for this book.

TEACHING THE SCRIPTURES

Book of the Law
(opened)

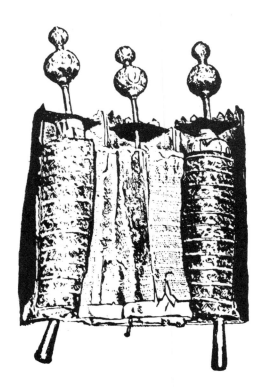

THE TORAH

HOW THE BIBLE WAS FORMED

"In the beginning was the Word . . . and the Word was God." - John 1:1

I. BOOK OF BOOKS
A. Library of 66 books
1. Old Testament - 39 books.
2. New Testament - 27 books.
B. Collection called
1. Bible (from Greek word <u>biblia</u> "little books").
2. Scriptures (from Latin <u>scriptura</u> "writings").
3. Canonical writings (from Greek <u>kanon</u> "rule"; books ruled genuine and inspired).

II. THE TWO TESTAMENTS OR COVENANTS
A. The Old Testament
1. Covenant (agreement, contract) with Abraham (Gen. 17:1-9).

Old Testament

B. The New Testament
1. Covenant foreseen by Jeremiah (Jer. 31:31-34) and fulfilled in Christ Jesus.

New Testament

C. Differences Between the Two Testaments
1. Language.
   a. Old Testament - Hebrew.
   b. New Testament - Greek.
2. Geography.
   a. Old Testament - Israel predominantly.
   b. New Testament - The "world".
3. Time.
   a. Old Testament - written over a period of ten to twenty centuries.
   b. New Testament - written within a 100 year period.
D. Unity Between the Two Testaments
1. Both Testaments concerned with the same God.
2. Both Testaments concerned with the same people.
3. The events of the Old Testament are seen as types of events in the New Testament.
4. The New Testament seen as the fulfillment of the Old.

III. MANUSCRIPTS

A. Writing
1. Earliest writing on clay tablets; later on skins (parchment).
2. Development of "papyrus" (from which comes the word paper).
3. Papyrus or skins glued into long strips that could be rolled up--"scroll".
4. Later strips bound together as leaves to make papyrus or parchment books (codex).
5. Hebrew written without vowels; Greek written in capitals and without spaces between words.
6. Laboriously and painstakingly copied by scribes.

B. Discovery of Printing in A.D. 1450
1. First book printed was the Latin Bible in 1456.
2. Chapters and verses first appeared in the English Geneva Bible A.D. 1560.

C. Discovery of the Dead Sea Scrolls in 1947
1. Previous earliest Greek manuscripts were from the fourth century A.D., and the oldest surviving complete Hebrew text was A.D. 1008.

IV. LITERATURE OF THE BIBLE (virtually every literary form)

A. Examples
1. Historical narratives (Books of Kings; Acts of Apostles).
2. Epic narratives (Joseph and his Brethren).
3. Victory songs (Song of Moses, Ex. 15; David's Psalm of Thanksgiving, II Samuel 22).
4. Laws (Exodus, Deuteronomy).
5. Songs (Psalms).
6. Autobiography (Jeremiah, Ezekiel).
7. Orations (Moses' addresses in Deuteronomy; Jesus' Sermon on the Mount).
8. Drama (Job).
9. Short stories (Ruth, Esther, Jonah).
10. Biography (Mark, Matthew, Luke).
11. Letters (of Paul).
12. Poetry (Isaiah, Amos, Micah).

V. EARLY TRANSLATIONS

A. Septuagint (285-132 B.C.)
1. Translation of the Old Testament into Greek--became the Bible of the early Christian Church.

B. Vulgate (A.D. 384-405)
1. Translation of the Septuagint into Latin by Jerome.

C. Translations into English
1. 1382 John Wyclif (translation of Vulgate into English).

2. 1525 William Tyndale (translation from Greek and Hebrew). English Bible
3. 1535 Myles Coverdale (first complete Bible in English; based on Latin, German, and Tyndale translations).
4. 1539 Great Bible (largely based on Tyndale and Coverdale; great size; installed in churches; first "official" version).
5. 1560 Geneva Bible (revision of Tyndale by William Whitingham and other Protestant scholars who fled to Geneva; small book, became the Bible of the home; division into chapters and verses).
6. 1568 Bishop's Bible (revision of Great Bible; appointed to be read in churches).
7. 1611 KING JAMES VERSION [KJV] or Authorized Version [AV] (a revision of Bishop's Bible which in time replaced the Bishop's Bible in the churches and the Geneva Bible in the homes; done by six committees of scholars using the best texts then available as well as European language version; language is Elizabethan, contemporary with Shakespeare; has been called "the noblest monument to English prose" for "its simplicity, its dignity, its power, its happy turns of expression, . . . the music of its cadences, and felicities of its rhythm"--written to be read aloud). King James Version

VI. MODERN TRANSLATIONS
A. Bible Scholarship
1. New manuscript finds and changing English usage led to further revisions.
2. More than 300 words in the King James Version are used in a sense substantially different from today's meaning.
B. Nineteenth Century Translations
1. 1881-1885 Revised Version [RV] (revision of the King James).
2. 1899 Twentieth Century New Testament.
3. 1901 American Standard Version [ASV] (variant of Revised Version).
C. Twentieth Century Translations Modern Translations
1. 1903 New Testament in Modern English (Weymouth).
2. 1913-1914 The Holy Bible, A New Translation (James Moffatt).
3. 1923-1927 The Bible, An American Translation (J. M. Powis Smith and Edgar J. Goodspeed).
4. 1946-1952 Revised Standard Version [RSV] (revision of the King James by American scholars).
5. 1958 The New Testament in Modern English (J. B. Phillips).
6. 1961-1970 The New English Bible [NEB] (British scholars; New Testament, Old Testament and Apocrypha; a fresh, lively rendition of the most ancient texts).

Teaching
the
Scriptures

Russell D. Robinson

New Edition
- revised and expanded -

one

7. 1966-1976 <u>Good News Bible</u> [TEV] (Today's English Version by American Bible Society).
8. 1973-1984 <u>New International Version</u> [NIV] (fresh, contemporary translation by scholars from United States, Canada, Australia and New Zealand by International Bible Society).
9. 1989 <u>The Revised English Bible</u> [REB] (major revision of The New English Bible).
10. 1989 <u>New Revised Standard Version</u> [NRSV] (new revision of the Revised Standard Version based on oldest and most reliable texts).

VII. COMPOSITION OF THE BIBLE

A. The Old Testament: The Hebrew Bible

Hebrew Bible

The Law

1. **The Law or Torah**.
   a. <u>Pentateuch</u> (Genesis, Exodus, Leviticus, Numbers, Deuteronomy). Probable oral transmission of stories, histories, maxims, laws, and songs for many centuries. Written compilation of history of the early period probably from the mid-ninth century on, first as separate northern and southern accounts, later combined, with several periods of later editorial revision, until the Torah was regarded as complete about 400 B.C. As finally edited these five books contain 613 different rules or laws.

Prophets

2. **The Prophets**.
   a. <u>The Former Prophets</u>: Joshua, Judges, Samuel, Kings. Joshua probably compiled in the manner of the Pentateuch. Judges, Samuel, Kings were probably separate stories written from the tenth century B.C., compiled as whole in Judah in the seventh and sixth centuries B.C.
   b. <u>The Latter Prophets</u>: Isaiah, Jeremiah, Ezekiel and The Twelve (minor prophets). Probably Isaiah, Jeremiah, and Ezekiel collections of sayings and writings; the minor prophets date from their own times (8th to 4th centuries B.C.); edited in post-exilic times with some interpolation. Completed by 200 B.C. and accepted as sacred.

Writings

3. **The Writings** (Ketubim, or Hagiographa, i.e. Sacred Writings).
   a. <u>Historical Books</u>: (Chronicles, Ezra, Nehemiah) by "the Chronicler".
   b. <u>Wisdom Books</u>: Job (anytime from 700 to 200 B.C.; edited late); Ecclesiastes (c. 250-150 B.C.); Proverbs (completed c. 200 B.C. from older collections).

      c. <u>Poetry</u>: Lamentations, Song of Solomon, c. 250 B.C.;
        Psalms, collection completed by about 100 B.C.

      d. <u>Stories</u>: Ruth (hard to date; probably post-exilic, c. 400
        B.C.); Esther (late, probably Maccabean period); Daniel
        (story combined with apocalyptic prophecy) c. 165 B.C.

  4. Canon of the Old Testament determined by Jewish Synod, c.
     A.D. 90.

B. Apocrypha Apocrypha

  1. Books written late, appearing in Greek Bible (the Septuagint)
and taken into the Latin Bible by Jerome, but excluded by
Jewish Synod as not sacred. Included in Roman Catholic
Bibles but not in Protestant Bibles (except sometimes as a
section between the Testaments).

  2. Jerome called them "apocryphal," that is, "hidden" or "secret"
evidently meaning of uncertain origin.

  3. Wisdom books: <u>Ecclesiasticus</u> c. 180 B.C.; <u>Wisdom of
Solomon</u>, perhaps first century A.D.; historical fiction: <u>Tobit</u>,
<u>Judith</u>, probably about the time of the Maccabees; history: <u>I
and II Maccabees</u>; there are also additions to Daniel and
Esther; <u>I and II Esdras</u>; <u>Baruch</u>; and the <u>Prayer of Manasseh</u>.

C. Pseudepigrapha Pseudepigrapha

  1. Various writings widely known and influential, mainly
apocalyptic, but never accepted as canon.

  2. Jude quotes from the pseudepigraphal <u>Book of Enoch</u> and
the <u>Assumption of Moses</u> in his letter.

  3. Includes such books as <u>Book of Jubilees</u>, the <u>Sybilline
Oracles</u>, <u>Book of Enoch</u>, <u>Book of the Secrets of Enoch</u>,
<u>Psalms of Solomon</u>, <u>Testaments of the Twelve Patriarchs</u>,
<u>Sayings of the Jewish Fathers</u>, etc.

D. New Testament New Testament

  1. Collections of "Sayings of Jesus" and perhaps biographical
narratives first written in Aramaic, the colloquial language of
Judea in the time of Jesus, are assumed.

  2. All New Testament books we have were written in Greek.

  3. Letters [Epistles] of Paul written during his missionary travels
after A.D. 49 and before his death (probably in A.D. 66).

  4. Synoptic Gospels (Mark, Matthew, Luke) and Acts probably
written between A.D. 65 to 85 or perhaps earlier.

  5. Gospel of John, Epistles of John, and Revelation probably
written A.D. 80 to 95 or perhaps somewhat earlier.

  6. James, Jude, I and II Peter, Hebrews written A.D. 50 to 130
(dates are very uncertain).

  7. Other books (such as <u>Gospel of Peter</u> and the <u>Epistle of
Barnabas</u>) were first circulated; gradually rejected. Canon of
27 books settled at Council of Carthage, A.D. 397.

Old Testament
The Law

VIII. ORDER OF BOOKS IN THE PROTESTANT OLD TESTAMENT

A. The Law or "Five Books of Moses"
1. Genesis (Beginnings; Abraham; Isaac, Jacob; Joseph).
2. Exodus (Moses leads out of Egypt; Commandments; Laws).
3. Leviticus (Priestly Laws, named after tribe of Levi).
4. Numbers (Record of Census--numberings; Wilderness Wanderings).
5. Deuteronomy (Recapitulation or repetition of Law).

Historical Books

B. Historical Writings
1. Joshua (Conquest of Canaan).
2. Judges (Settlement of Canaan).
3. Ruth (Story of David's great-grandmother).
4. I Samuel (Samuel; Saul; David).
5. II Samuel (King David).
6. I Kings (King Solomon; Two Rival Kingdoms; Elijah).
7. II Kings (Elisha; Fall of Israel and Judah).

C. Later Historical Writings
1. I Chronicles (Saul: David).
2. II Chronicles (Solomon; Two Kingdoms; Captivity).
3. Ezra (Captivity [Exile] and Return).
4. Nehemiah (Rebuilding Jerusalem).
5. Esther (Hebrew Girl in Persian Court).

Poetical Books

D. Poetry
1. Job (a Poetic Drama).
2. Psalms (Songs and Hymns).
3. Proverbs (Wise Sayings).
4. Ecclesiastes (a Sermon in Poetry).
5. Song of Solomon (a Love Song).

Prophetical Books

E. Major Prophets
1. Isaiah (Ch. 1--39, 8th century B.C. in Judah; Ch. 40--66, 6th century).
2. Jeremiah (7th and 6th centuries in Judah).
3. Lamentations (7th century, attributed to Jeremiah).
4. Ezekiel (6th century during Captivity [Exile]).
5. Daniel (6th century during Captivity).

F. Minor Prophets--the Twelve

1. Hosea	7. Nahum
2. Joel	8. Habakkuk
3. Amos	9. Zephaniah
4. Obadiah	10. Haggai
5. Jonah	11. Zechariah
6. Micah	12. Malachi

[Roman Catholic Bibles and Eastern Orthodox Bibles contain the same books listed above with the addition of Apocryphal books which are usually interspersed among the Old Testament writings.]

IX. ORDER OF BOOKS IN THE NEW TESTAMENT
    A. Biographies of Jesus--the Gospels
        1. Matthew
        2. Mark
        3. Luke
        4. John
    B. History of Early Church
        1. Acts
    C. Letters of Paul to Churches
        1. Romans   6. Philippians
        2. I Corinthians   7. Colossians
        3. II Corinthians   8. I Thessalonians
        4. Galatians   9. II Thessalonians
        5. Ephesians
    D. Letters of Paul to Individuals
        1. I Timothy
        2. II Timothy
        3. Titus
        4. Philemon
    E. Other Letters by Early Christians
        1. Hebrews   5. I John
        2. James   6. II John
        3. I Peter   7. III John
        4. II Peter   8. Jude
    F. The Apocalypse
        1. Revelation

X. BIBLE STUDY AIDS
    A. Bibles
        1. Translations (excellent for comparative study).
        2. Reference Bibles (with textual references related to Scriptural passages).
        3. Study Bibles (with study helps concurrent with the text; frequently highly interpretive).
    B. Bible Concordances
        1. All words arranged alphabetically with references where words appear.
        2. Usually also contain lexicons of Greek and Hebrew.
    C. Bible Dictionaries
        1. Alphabetical articles by names of people, places, words, books, events, etc.
    D. Bible Commentaries
        1. Commentary by scholars by chapter and verse through the Bible.
    E. Bible Atlas
        1. Extensive maps of various Bible periods.
        2. Concise historical narrative.

Margin notes:

New Testament

Gospels

Early Christianity

Letters of Paul

Other Letters

Apocalypse

Bible Aids

Bibles

Concordances

Dictionaries

Commentaries

Atlas

Scroll

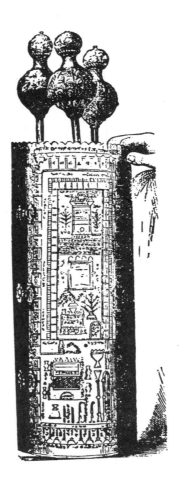

BOOK OF THE LAW
(closed)

INTRODUCTION
TO THE SCRIPTURES (GENESIS)

"All things were made by him; and without him was not anything made that
was made."   -John 1:3

I. INTRODUCTION TO THE BIBLE
A. Prose Poem
    1. A poetic metaphoric description of the illumination of human
consciousness--of the coming of revelation to thought: the
realization that man is created in the image and likeness of
God and that God's creation is good, "and the Spirit of God
moved upon the face of the waters." Metaphors adapted
from Babylonian creation myth. | Creation

B. Poem written about 400 B.C.
    1. Written as preface to the Pentateuch or Book of the Law.

C. The Revelation of God's Creation (Gen. 1:1--2:3) | Perception of Spiritual Truth
    1. Let there be light: and there was light . . . and God divided
the light from the darkness . . .(1:1-5).

    2. Let there be a firmament . . . and let it divide the waters . . .
which were under the firmament from the waters which were
above the firmament (1:6-8). | Understanding Separates False

    3. Let the waters . . . be gathered together unto one place, and
let the dry land appear . . . Let the earth bring forth grass, the
herb . . . and the fruit . . . whose seed is in itself (1:9-13). | Resurrection of Thought

    4. Let there be lights in the firmament . . . and God made two
great lights . . . he made the stars also (1:14-19). | Illumination of Thought

    5. Let the waters bring forth abundantly the moving creature . . .
and fowl that may fly over the earth . . . And God blessed
them saying, Be fruitful and multiply . . . (1:20-23). | Discernment of Good Creation

    6. Let the earth bring forth the living creature . . . Let us make
man in our image, and after our likeness: and let them have
dominion over the fish . . . and over the fowl . . . and over the
cattle, and over all the earth, and over every creeping thing . .
. So God created man in his own image . . . male and female .
. . and God said unto them, Be fruitful and multiply, and
replenish the earth, and subdue it: and have dominion . . .
And God saw everything that he had made, and, behold, it
was very good. . . . (1:24-31). | Discernment of Man as Image With Dominion

    7. Thus the heavens and the earth were finished . . . and God . . .
rested on the seventh day from all the work which he had
made . . . (2:1-3). | Realization Complete

two

II. AN ALLEGORY

A. Written in the Tenth Century B.C.

1. Written some 600 years before the opening prose poem.

Allegory

2. An allegorical explanation of the human condition. In startling contradiction of the good creation, it depicts mankind (Adam), a disobedient, confused, self-deceived, alienated, absurd mortal beguiled by "the serpent".

B. The Human Mind and its Self-deception (Gen. 2:4--4:26)

Confusion of Thought

1. . . . But there went up a mist from the earth, and watered the whole face of the ground. (2:4-6).

Life in Matter

2. And the Lord God formed man of the dust of the ground, and breathed into his nostrils the breath of life . . . (2:7).

Dualism of Human Mind

3. And the Lord God planted a garden eastward in Eden; and there he put the man . . . and out of the ground made the Lord God to grow every tree . . .; the tree of life also in the midst of the garden, and the tree of the knowledge of good and evil. And a river went out of Eden to water the garden . . . and it became four heads . . . Pison . . . Gihon . . . Hiddekel . . . and . . . Euphrates . . . And the Lord God commanded the man, . . . of the tree of knowledge of good and evil, thou shalt not eat of it . . . (2:8-17).

Self-deception

4. . . . out of the ground the Lord God formed every beast . . . and every fowl . . . and whatsoever Adam called every living creature, that was the name thereof. . . . And the Lord God caused a deep sleep to fall upon Adam . . . and he took one of his ribs . . . and . . . made he a woman . . . Now the serpent was more subtle than any beast of the field . . . and when the woman saw that the tree was good for food . . . she took of the fruit thereof, and did eat, and gave also to her husband with her; and he did eat . . . (2:18--3:7).

Self-knowledge

5. And the Lord God called unto Adam, and said unto him, Where art thou? . . . And the man said, The woman . . . beguiled me, and I did eat. And the Lord God said unto the serpent, . . . I will put enmity between thee and the woman, and between thy seed and her seed; it shall bruise thy head, and thou shalt bruise his heel. (3:8-15).

Man Separated from God

6. Unto the woman he said, I will greatly multiply thy sorrow . . . And unto Adam he said, . . . in the sweat of thy face shalt thou eat bread . . . Therefore the Lord God sent him forth from the garden of Eden, to till the ground . . . So he drove out the man . . . (3:16-24).

Depravity

7. And Adam knew Eve . . . and she . . . bare Cain . . . and Abel. . . . Cain rose up against Abel his brother, and slew him. And the Lord said unto Cain, Where is Abel thy brother? And he said, I know not: Am I my brother's keeper? . . . And Cain went out from the presence of the Lord, and dwelt in the land of Nod . . . (4:1-26).

III. GENERATIONS OF "ADAM" (Hebrew for "mankind" or "red earth")   Adam
   A. Ten Generations
      1. From Adam to Noah: (1) Adam, (2) Seth, (3) Enos, (4)   Enoch
        Cainan, (5) Mahalaleel, (6) Jared, (7) Enoch - Gen. 5:21-24,
        (8) Methuselah, (9) Lamech, and (10) Noah.
      2. Names and years given may refer to a family or tribe, or the
        tribe and its chief, instead of individual people. There is a
        Chaldean record of "ten dynasties before the flood." Names
        of dynasties are similar to those in Genesis 5.

IV. NOAH (Gen. 6--10)
   A. An Ancient Story of a Catastrophic Flood and Few Survivors
      1. To illustrate God's protection of the righteous, that God is
        just.
      2. There are records of an extensive deluge recorded in legends
        of Mesopotamia and other ancient peoples as well as the
        Hebrews, particularly the "Epic of Gilgamish" which tells of a
        man named Utnapishtim.
   B. The Story of Noah
      1. "Noah was a just man and perfect in his generations, and   Noah
        Noah walked with God . . . And God said unto Noah . . .
        Make thee an ark . . . And the flood was forty days upon the   Ark
        earth; and the waters increased, and bare up the ark, and it
        was lift up above the earth. . . . And the ark went upon the   Flood
        face of the waters.
      2. . . . And God remembered Noah and every living thing . . .
        that was with him in the ark . . . and the waters decreased . . .
        Noah opened the window of the ark . . . he sent forth a raven
        . . . also he sent forth a dove . . . and, lo, in her mouth was an   Raven
        olive leaf plucked off: so Noah knew that the waters were   Dove
        abated. . . . And Noah went forth . . . And Noah builded an
        altar. . . .
      3. And God spake unto Noah, . . . behold, I establish my
        covenant with you. . . . I do set my bow in the cloud and it   Covenant
        shall be for a token of a covenant between me and the
        earth. . . .
      4. And the sons of Noah, that went forth of the ark, were Shem,   Shem
        and Ham, and Japheth: and Ham is the father of Canaan.   Ham
        These are the three sons of Noah: and of them was the whole   Japheth
        earth overspread. . . . And Noah . . . said, Cursed be Canaan   Canaan
        . . . God shall enlarge Japheth, and he shall dwell in the tents
        of Shem, and Canaan shall be his servant."
   C. Explanation of Peoples of Earth
      1. Shem considered ancestor of Arab peoples; Ham of African
        peoples, and Japheth of northern peoples. Note curse was
        not on Ham but on Canaan, ancient enemy of Israel.

11

Tower of Babel

Shem

Parchment Case
and Scrolls

V. THE TOWER OF BABEL (Gen. 11:1-9)

A. Explanation of Divisions of Mankind

1. An ancient story of abandoning of the building of a ziggurat, told to explain the origin of languages and cultural differences.

B. The Story of Babel (Hebrew word for "Babylon")

1. "And the whole earth was of one language, and . . . they found a plain in the land of Shinar [Sumer], and they dwelt there. . . And they said, Go to, let us build us a city and a tower, whose top may reach unto heaven . . . And the Lord said, . . . let us go down, and there confound their language, that they may not understand one another's speech. So the Lord scattered them abroad. . . . Therefore is the name of it called Babel."

VI. GENERATIONS OF SHEM (Hebrew for "name")

A. Ten Generations

1. From Shem to Abraham: (1) Shem, (2) Arphaxad, (3) Salah, (4) Eber, [Heber, Hebrew, Habiru], (5) Peleg, (6) Reu, (7) Serug, (8) Nahor, (9) Terah, (10) Abraham.

JOB - A SEARCHER FOR GOD

"Oh that I knew where I might find him!" -Job 23:3

I. THE BOOK OF JOB
A. Great Literature
1. The supreme example of Wisdom literature.
2. Stands with Deutero-Isaiah (Isa. 40-66) as one of the greatest works of literary art in the Old Testament.
3. Impossible to date; the prose-prologue and epilogue are very old (possibly a story of the Job of Gen. 46:13, also referred to as a man of righteousness in Ezek. 14:14-20; poem probably dates from late in seventh century, with parts (such as Elihu's speech) added still later; final form in fifth century.
4. Literary parallels to Job may be found in Near Eastern literature as early as 2000 B.C. in Sumerian, Babylonian, and Ugaritic writings.

II. PROBLEMS WITH WHICH THE BOOK DEALS
A. Why Do the Innocent Suffer? (problem of evil)
B. Does Job Have a Right to Question God? (problem of inquiry)
C. What is Man's Relationship With God? (problem of relationship)

III. PROSE PROLOGUE (Job 1:1--2:13)
A. Scene Shifts Between the Court of Heaven and the Land of Uz
1. Conversation about Job between the Lord and Satan (in Hebrew Satan means "the adversary").
B. "The Adversary" Tests Job's Fidelity and Uprightness
1. Job is stripped of wealth, children, and health.

IV. THE DRAMATIC POEM (Job 3:1--42:6)
A. Scene: the Ash Heap
B. Cast of Characters:
1. **Job**, a righteous man who meets calamity and seeks God.
2. **Eliphaz**, speaks from the orthodox view of spirituality.
3. **Bildad**, speaks from traditional view of intellectual piety.
4. **Zophar**, speaks from what he regards as practical dogmatism.
5. **Elihu**, a youthful observer.
6. **God**, the Voice out of the Whirlwind, speaks directly to Job.

Job

Problem

Prologue

Cast

C. Job's Lament (3:1-26)

    1. "Let the day perish wherein I was born, . . . for the thing which I greatly feared is come upon me, and that which I was afraid of is come unto me".

Eliphaz
Bildad
Zophar

D. Eliphaz, Bildad, Zophar, the Three Friends, Speak to Job in Three Series of Speeches (4:1--28:28)

    1. In the first round of speeches, Job's friends argue with Job in terms of God's justice and righteousness (4:1--14:22).

    2. In the second round of speeches, the friends argue generally concerning the fate of wicked men (15:1--21:34).

    3. In the third round of speeches, they accuse Job directly of great sins (22:1--28:28).

    4. They present the view that suffering is God's punishment for wrong-doing, and this accounts for Job's suffering; they declare there is an infinite distance between God and man.

    5. Job declares his innocence of wrong-doing and denies this orthodox explanation; he seeks to know God, to speak to God, to reason with God, to ask God.

    6. His friends condemn this desire; he should be content with orthodox answers.

    7. Job says of his friends, "Miserable comforters are ye all."

E. Job's Final Response to their Arguments--the Oath of Clearing (29:1--31:40)

    1. Job clears himself of wrong-doing and pleads his innocence and his right to present his case before God.

Elihu

F. Elihu, One of the Silent Spectators to the Argument Now Speaks (32:1--37:24)

    1. Despite his eloquence, he adds little new to the debate.

    2. As he speaks, a terrifying storm comes up.

Voice

G. Climax of the Poem: Job's Spiritual Experience (38:1--42:6)

    1. God speaks directly to Job in a voice out of the whirlwind.

    2. Job's questioning is silenced by the revelation of the might, majesty, and glory of God.

    3. Job gratefully responds, "I have heard of thee by the hearing of the ear: but now mine eye seeth thee."

V. EPILOGUE (Job 42:7-17)

Job's Reward

A. God Rewards Job's Seeking

    1. The servile reverence of the friends had distorted the facts in order to magnify God.

    2. Job is restored to health and prosperity and he prays for his friends.

B. The Lesson of Job

    1. The problems posed by the poem have not been answered directly, but the poem is a vindication of the right of such inquiry. Job's trial ends in triumph.

PRE-HISTORY - BEFORE ABRAHAM

"The light shineth in darkness; and the darkness comprehended it not."
-John 1:5

I. **ABOUT 500,000 YEARS AGO (or perhaps 1 million years ago)**
  A. **Human Beings Appear**
    1. Discover fire; develop tools; cook; kill for food.
    2. People live an essentially non-human animal life.

II. **ABOUT 35,000 TO 10,000 YEARS AGO**
  A. **Development of Agriculture**
    1. Domestication of animals.
    2. Transition from stone to iron tools.
  B. **Art and Religion Appears**
    1. Rituals, ceremonials for burial, etc.
    2. People live a primitive human life.

III. **ABOUT 6,000 TO 4,000 YEARS AGO**
  A. **Rise of Cities and Civilization**
    1. Development of idea of division of labor.
    2. Invention of human slavery.
    3. Flowering of arts, sciences, religion, government (made possible for the elite because the masses [the slaves] did the work).
    4. Civilizations first arose on the banks of four rivers: the Tigris/Euphrates, Nile, Indus and Yellow rivers.
  B. **Sumer and Egypt**
    1. Development of writing, arithmetic, calendar, money and credit, the wheel, representational art, monumental architecture--all one thousand years or more before Abraham in ancient Sumer (c. 3000 B.C.).
    2. Contact between Egypt and Sumer from earliest times across the "Fertile Crescent."
    3. Pyramids built in Egypt (c. 2700 B.C.).
    4. Egypt ruled by Hyksos (Shepherd Kings) c. 1720-1570 B.C., around the time of Patriarchs.
  C. **Ancient City of Ur ("Ur of the Chaldees") in Sumer**
    1. 100 per cent literacy, well-established schools, libraries, and art museums, and a religion of many gods, chief of which was Sin, the moon god.

Fire

Domestication
of Animals
Iron Tools

Rise of
Civilization

Sumer

Ur

Ebla

D. Ancient City of Ebla
  1. 15,000 clay tablets found in Syria in 1974 describing life in
  2500 B.C.

Jericho

E. Ancient City of Jericho
  1. Often called "oldest walled city in the world" dating from 8000
  B.C.

Early Writing

Patriarchs

IV. GENEALOGY

Adam ("mankind")
(Eve)
├────────────────────┬──────────────────┤
Seth   Abel   Cain
│
Noah (10th from Adam)
├────────────────────┬──────────────────┤
Shem   Japheth   Ham
│   Canaan
Abraham (10th from Shem)
(Sarah)   (Hagar)
├───────────────────────────────────────┤
Isaac   Ishmael
(Rebekah)
├───────────────────────────────────────┤
Jacob—ISRAEL   Esau
│
Children of Israel

16

FROM ABRAHAM TO MOSES
(circa 2000 B.C. to 1500 B.C.)

"I am the God of thy father, the God of Abraham, the God of Isaac, and the God of Jacob"   -Exodus 3:6

I. THE PATRIARCHS (circa 2100-1700 B.C.)
A. Abraham
1. Abram [Abraham] and Sarai [Sarah] and others leave "Ur of the Chaldees" for Haran in upper Mesopotamia (Gen. 11:31).
2. Depart from Haran for Canaan (12:1-8).
3. To Egypt because of famine (12:9-20).
4. Return to Bethel (13:1-5).
5. Abram and Lot separate (13:6-18).
6. Abram rescues Lot and pays tribute to Melchizedek (Gen. 14).
7. Abram's dream (Gen. 15).
8. Ishmael born to Hagar (Gen. 16).
9. Abram settles in Hebron. Abram's Covenant with God (Gen. 17:1-9), and circumcision instituted (17:10-27). Names changed to Abraham and Sarah (17:5, 15).
10. "Three men" appear to Abraham (18:1-22).
11. Abraham pleads for sparing Sodom (18:23-33).
12. Sodom destroyed and Lot saved (Gen. 19).
13. Abraham heals Abimelech (20:17).
14. Isaac born and Ishmael sent away (Gen. 21).
15. Test of Abraham's faith to sacrifice Isaac (22:1-13).
16. Burial place (Gen. 23).

B. Isaac (Son of Abraham)
1. Oriental courtship and marriage to Rebekah (Gen. 24).
2. Twins (Jacob and Esau) born to Isaac and Rebekah (25:19-26).
3. Jacob takes advantage of brother; takes Esau's birthright (25:27-34).
4. Isaac refuses to fight over wells (26:17-22).
5. Isaac makes treaty of peace (26:23-33).

Abraham
Sarah

Hagar
Ishmael

Covenant

Isaac
Rebekah

Jacob
Esau

17

Migration of
Abraham

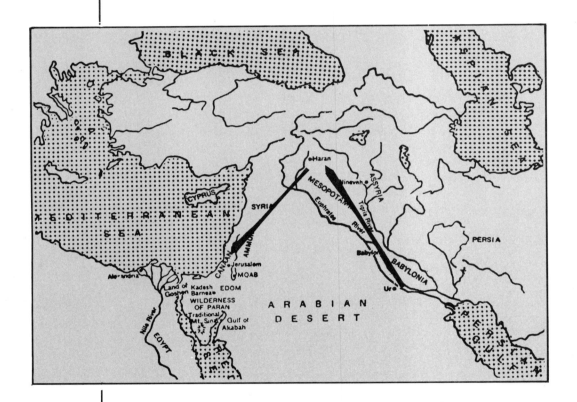

**THE MIGRATION OF ABRAHAM
ACROSS THE FERTILE CRESCENT**

C. Jacob (Son of Isaac)

1. Jacob and Rebekah trick Isaac into giving Jacob the blessing instead of Esau (Gen. 27:1--28:9) and Jacob has to flee to his Uncle Laban in Haran.
2. Jacob's vision at Bethel on the trip to Haran (28:10-22)--the ladder to heaven.
3. Marriage to Leah and Rachel; eleven sons born to Jacob in Haran (Gen. 29; 30).
4. Twenty years later, separation from Laban (Gen. 31).
5. Jacob returns home still fearing Esau (Gen. 32:1-23).
6. Jacob's wrestling at Peniel (32:24-30)--name changed to Israel.
7. Friendly meeting with Esau (Gen. 33).
8. Settles at Bethel (35:1-15).
9. A twelfth son (Benjamin) born and Rachel dies (35:16-19).

II. THE TWELVE SONS OF JACOB--THE CHILDREN OF ISRAEL

A. By Leah:
1. Reuben (1)
2. Simeon (2)
3. Levi (3)
4. Judah (4)
5. Issachar (9)
6. Zebulum (10)
7. Dinah, a daughter.

B. By Bilhah, Rachel's maid:
1. Dan (5)
2. Naphtali (6)

C. By Zilpah, Leah's maid:
1. Gad (7)
2. Asher (8)

D. By Rachel:
1. Joseph (11)
2. Benjamin (12)

E. Joseph
1. Cast into pit and sold into Egypt (Gen. 37)--age 17.
2. Served Potiphar for 13 years (39:1-19).
3. Falsely imprisoned (39:20--40:23).
4. Becomes viceroy (prime minister) of Egypt (Gen. 41).
5. Sons of Joseph: Manasseh and Ephraim (41:50-52).
6. Joseph and his brothers (Gen. 42--45).
7. The whole family of Jacob (Israel) settles in Egypt (Gen. 46, 47).

III. CHILDREN OF ISRAEL IN EGYPT (about 1700 B.C.)

A. About 400 years in Egypt

Jacob
(Israel)

Children of Israel

Joseph

In Egypt

1. Jacob's prophecies concerning his sons (Gen. 48, 49).
2. Passing of Joseph (Gen. 50).
3. Later enslavement and cruel treatment (Ex. 1:8-22).

Contemporary Events

IV. CONTEMPORARY EVENTS

    A. During the 500 years from Abraham to Moses, elsewhere in the world

      1. Hammurabi issues Law Code in Babylon; rise of Babylon.
      2. Height of Indus civilization at Harappa and Mohenjo-daro.
      3. Middle Kingdom in Egypt.
      4. Minoan civilization on Crete.
      5. Mycenaeans reach Greece from the north and Mycenaean civilization begins.
      6. Shun dynasty in China.
      7. Stonehenge in England.
      8. Bronze Age in Europe.

Setting up the Tent of Meeting

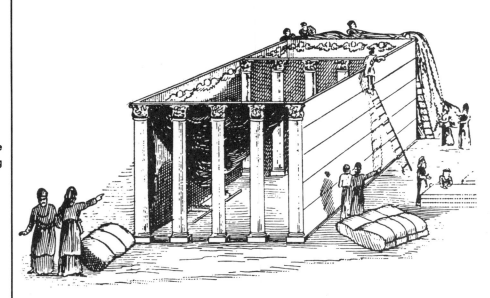

THE HOLY PLACE AND THE HOLY OF HOLIES

FROM MOSES TO DAVID

(circa 1500 B.C. to 1000 B.C.)

"Hear, O Israel: The Lord our God is one Lord: And thou shalt love the Lord thy God with all thine heart, and with all thy soul, and with all thy might."
-Deuteronomy 6:4, 5

I. MOSES AND THE EXODUS (about 1300 B.C.)
  A. Birth and Youth--to His Call (Ex. 1-4)   Moses
    1. Moses rescued and raised in Pharaoh's palace (2:1-10).
    2. Killing an Egyptian and flight to land of Midian (2:11-15).
    3. Marriage to daughter of priest of Midian (2:16-22).
    4. Call of Moses, experience at the burning bush (3:1-20); I AM THAT I AM.
    5. God's presence and power revealed to Moses (4:1-18).
    6. Association with Aaron (4:28-31), brother of Moses.
  B. Rescue of Israelites (Ex. 5--15)
    1. Pharaoh refuses to let Israelites leave (Ex. 5).
    2. Covenant renewed with Moses (6:1-13).   Covenant
    3. Contest with Pharaoh--the Plagues (Ex. 7--11).
    4. Passover instituted and flight to the Red Sea (Ex. 12, 13).   Escape from Egypt
    5. Crossing of the Red Sea (Ex. 14).
    6. Moses' Song of Victory (15:1-21).
  C. The Covenant on Sinai (the first year of wandering)
    1. The trek to Sinai--amid murmuring.
      a. Manna and quails (Ex. 16).
      b. Water from rock (17:1-7).
      c. Enemies overcome (17:8-16).
      d. Reunion with Jethro (18:1-12).
    2. Moses establishes a government (18:13-26).
    3. The great theophany on Mt. Sinai (Mt. Horeb) (Ex. 19).
      a. **THE TEN COMMANDMENTS**, the tables of stone, (20:1-17); the moral law which forbids (1) polytheism, (2) idolatry, (3) blasphemy, (4) irreverence, (5) inhumanity, (6) murder, (7) adultery, (8) stealing, (9) lying, (10) coveting -- 10 evils that separate man from God and man from man   Ten Commandments
      b. The Book of the Covenant (Ex. 20:22--23:19)
      c. Further Instructions (23:20--24:8)

Tent of Meeting

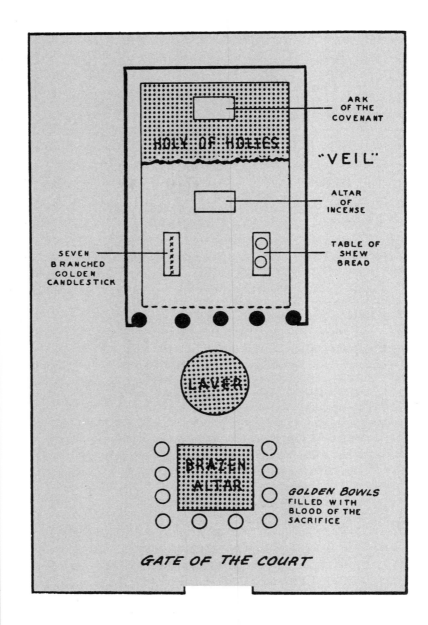

DIAGRAM OF
THE TABERNACLE OF MOSES

(TENT OF MEETING)

4. Moses establishes a system of worship (the tent of meeting, or "tabernacle in the wilderness") (Ex. 25--31; 35--40).

5. **Tent of Meeting--Seven Steps in Worship.**

Entrance
Symbolizing
Desire to Worship

a. **ONE.** Entrance on one side only for people to enter for worship.

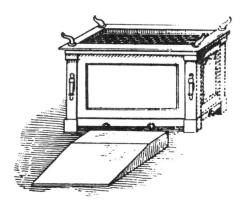

Brazen Altar
Symbolizing
Sacrifice of
Cherished Beliefs

b. **TWO.** Brazen altar for the burnt offerings which was surrounded by bowls to be filled with the blood of the sacrifice.

Laver
Symbolizing
Purification
of Thought

c. **THREE**. Laver in which priest could wash after the sacrifice.

[Only priests were permitted beyond this point to enter the inner sanctuary in which were three pieces of furniture.]

Seven-branched
Candlestick
Symbolizing
Spiritual
Illumination

d. **FOUR**. Seven-branched golden candlestick.

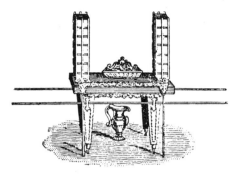

Shew Bread
Symbolizing
Spiritual Supply

e. **FIVE.** Table of Shewbread with twelve loaves of unleavened bread in two rows, six in each row.

Incense
Symbolizing
Gratitude
and Praise

f. **SIX.** Altar of incense before the veil or curtain.

VEIL

VEIL
Symbolizing
Final Barrier

[Only once a year, on the Day of Atonement, was a high priest (archpriest), wearing Urim and Thummim, permitted beyond the veil into the "Holy of Holies"].

HOLY OF HOLIES

Ark
Symbolizing
At-one-ment
With God

g. **SEVEN.** Ark of the Covenant (a box containing the two tables of stone [Commandments]). On the top of the box was the "mercy seat" between the cherubim.

Golden Calf

6. The Golden Calf.
   a. Backsliding and Moses' anger and breaking of the tables (Ex. 32--33).
   b. Second set of tables (Ex. 34) (thought to be actually earlier than those given in Ex. 20).

Wilderness
Wanderings

D. The Wandering in the Wilderness--from Sinai to the Wilderness of Paran (the second year)
1. Advance from Sinai with the Ark; a pillar of cloud by day and of fire by night (Num. 9:15-23).
2. Murmurings, quails and plague (Num. 11).
   a. Moses heals Miriam of leprosy after she and Aaron attempt to usurp his leadership (Num. 12).
3. Attempt to enter Canaan from south; spies sent out; only Joshua and Caleb brought back encouraging report (Num. 13).
4. Condemned to forty years of wandering; defeat in battle (Num. 14).

E. Thirty-eight More Years of Desert Wanderings
1. Sojourn at Kadesh in the Wilderness of Zin (Num. 20:1).
2. Waters of Meribah, water from the rock; Moses' sin of pride (20:2-13).
3. New attempt to enter Canaan; passage through Edom refused (20:14-21).
4. Fiery serpent bites healed (21:5-9).
5. Passage through Moab (21:10-35; 25; 31).

Balaam and Balak

6. The Moabite King Balak and the Mesopotamian diviner, Balaam (Num. 22--24).

F. Pisgah (or Mt. Nebo)
1. Appointment of Joshua as successor (Num. 27:12-23).
2. Allotment of the tribes (Num. 32, 34, 35).

3. The farewell orations of Moses: Deuteronomy (the second giving of the Law).
    a. Restatement of Ten Commandments after 40 years (Deut. 5:6-21).
    b. <u>Shema</u> meaning "Hear" (Deut. 6:4-9). Used in worship.
    c. Farewell orations (Deut. 32, 33).
4. Moses passes on before the Israelites enter the Promised Land of Canaan (Deut. 34).

Restatement of Commandments

Shema

II. THE PENTATEUCH (TORAH OR LAW)
A. Sources

Pentateuch

1. Books are attributed to Moses, but actually are the result of over five centuries of literary activity.
2. Four narratives ("J", "E", "D", and "P") were edited, combined, interwoven, and added to by priestly editors around 400 B.C. to make Genesis, Exodus, Numbers, Leviticus, Deuteronomy.
3. "J"--originating in the southern kingdom of Judah in the 10th century. Uses <u>Jehovah</u> (more correctly "<u>Yahweh</u>") for Deity. (King James Version translates it "Lord God").

J Document

4. "E"--originating in the northern kingdom of Israel (Ephraim) in the 9th century. Uses <u>Elohim</u> for Deity (K.J.V. translates it "God"). JE combined about 650 B.C.

E Document

5. "D"--originating in Judah by prophetic writers in the 7th century; Deuteronomy. JED combined in the 6th century.

D Document

6. "P"--written by priestly writers between 550 and 500 B.C. revising earlier sources from a priestly viewpoint; largely ritualistic and legalistic; Leviticus, including the earlier Holiness Code (Lev. 17--26). JEDP combined as Torah or Law, in the 5th century containing total of 613 specific laws.

P Document

7. This pattern of authorship also true of Joshua, and probably to some extent, Judges, I and II Samuel, and I and II Kings, as there is evidence of two or more source documents in these works, although mostly the work of "D".

III. JOSHUA (about 1250-1225 B.C.)
A. The Conquest of Canaan

Joshua

1. Commissioning Joshua as Moses' successor; crossing the Jordan river; invasion of Canaan and capture of Jericho (Josh. 1--6).
2. Conquer most of Canaan; destruction of Ai (Josh. 7--12).
3. Land divided between the twelve tribes (Josh. 13--21). Land given to every tribe except the tribe of Levi--the priestly tribe. The tribe of Joseph received a portion for each son: Manasseh and Ephraim were considered as two tribes to make twelve. Levites dwelt in all tribes to serve as priests.
4. Joshua's final advice (Josh. 22--24).

six

Promised Land

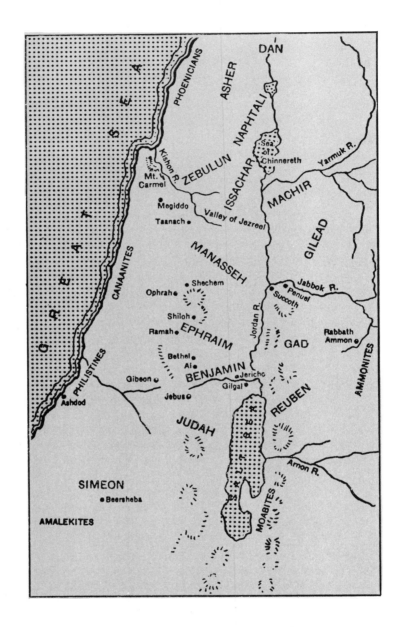

**THE TWELVE TRIBES
IN THE
PROMISED LAND OF CANAAN**

IV. JUDGES (about 1225-1020 B.C.) Judges
   A. The Book
      1. A disconnected treatment of some events over a two-hundred year period between Joshua and Samuel.
      2. The "judges" were military heroes and leaders who rallied the tribes at crucial periods against enemies.
   B. Some of the Judges
      1. Deborah (the woman judge) and Barak (Judges 4 and 5). Deborah
      2. Gideon (Judges 6, 7, 8). Gideon
      3. Abimelech, the usurper, and Jotham's parable (8:29--9:57). Abimelech
      4. Jephthah and daughter (11:6-12). Jephthah
      5. Samson (Judges 13:24--16:31). Samson

V. RUTH Ruth
   A. A Historical Romance
      1. Ruth was a Moabitess, the great-grandmother of David.
      2. Story of her relationship to her mother-in-law and her marriage to Boaz.
      3. Probably written sometime after 400 B.C. as a protest against the rigid inter-marriage prohibitions of Ezra.

VI. SAMUEL Samuel
   A. Last and Greatest of the Judges
      1. Presented to the Lord to be raised by the high priest, Eli (I Sam. 1:20--2:11).
      2. Corruption at shrine at Shiloh (2:12-36).
      3. Hears the voice of God (3:1-18).
      4. Becomes well-known (3:19-22).
      5. Ark of Covenant stolen by Philistines and returned (I Sam. 4--6).
      6. Assembly at Mizpeh; Samuel as judge on circuit (I Sam. 7).
      7. Israelites desire a king (I Sam. 8).

VII. SAUL AND DAVID (about 1020-1005 B.C.)
   A. Reign of King Saul Saul
      1. Saul chosen and anointed by Samuel (I Sam. 9, 10).
      2. Saul's reign begins (I Sam. 11).
      3. Samuel's charge to Israel and the king (I Sam. 12).
      4. Successes and failures of Saul as king (I Sam. 13, 14, 15).
   B. Young Manhood of David David
      1. Samuel secretly anoints David as Saul's successor (16:1-13).
      2. David becomes Saul's harpist and armor bearer (16:14-23).
      3. David defeats Goliath (17:1-51).
      4. Saul jealously tries to kill David (I Sam. 18).

5. David's "outlaw" years with Saul in pursuit.
   a. Saul's son, Jonathan, becomes David's friend (I Sam. 18--20).
   b. Saul pursues David (I Sam. 21--23).
6. David refuses to kill Saul (I Sam. 24).
   a. David helped by Abigail (I Sam. 25).
   b. Saul again spared by David (I Sam. 26).
   c. Shelter with Philistines (I Sam. 27).
7. Saul consults spiritualist at Endor to contact dead Samuel (I Sam. 28).
8. David's success in battle (I Sam. 29, 30).
9. Battle of Gilboa; Saul kills himself and the kingdom splits in two (I Sam. 31).
10. David's lament for Saul and Jonathan (II Sam. 1).

VIII. THE PROMISED LAND
A. Differences Between North and South
1. History, Culture, Soil, Climate, and Geographical Location
B. The North (Israel)
1. In the midst of Fertile Crescent.
2. Close ties with neighboring lands.
3. Adequate rainfall to grow grain, grapes, olives.
4. Rich pastures to support cattle and farming.
C. The South (Judah)
1. Dry, little rainfall, barren soil.
2. Imported more than it exported.
3. People mostly shepherds rather than farmers.
4. More insulated from its neighbors.
D. To Maintain a Union
1. Two lands needed a strong ruler.

IX. CONTEMPORARY EVENTS
A. During the 500 Years Between Moses and David,
When Canaan Was Being Settled by the Hebrews, Elsewhere in the World:
1. The Trojan War in Greece (later immortalized by Homer).
2. Rise of Shang civilization in China.
3. Beginnings of Mayan civilization in central America.
4. Development of Hinduism in India.
5. Ikhnaton of Egypt sets up one god (Aton, the sun god); his successor Tutankhamen reinstates earlier deities.
6. Phoenicians predominant trading power on Mediterranean.
7. Mexican sun pyramid.

Jonathan

Abigail

Canaan

Contemporary Events

FROM DAVID TO DANIEL

(circa 1000 B.C. to 500 B.C.)

"What doth the Lord require of thee, but to do justly, and to love mercy, and to walk humbly with thy God?"   -Micah 6:6

I. KING DAVID (about 1005-965 B.C.)   King David
   A. Consolidation of the Kingdom
      1. David chosen king over Judah at Hebron (II Sam. 2:1-3).
      2. Rival kingdom of Israel set up by Ishbaal (Ishbosheth), son of Saul; Civil War followed (II Sam. 2--4).
      3. David king of Israel and Judah at age 37 (II Sam. 5:1-4).
   B. The United Kingdom
      1. Capture of Jerusalem which is made the capital (II Sam. 5).
      2. Ark brought to Jerusalem; David's dancing; Temple to be   Temple
built in Jerusalem on Mount Zion but not by David (II Sam. 6, 7).
      3. Conquests of David, partly carried out by Joab as David's   Joab
commander (II Sam. 5, 8, 10):
         a. Conquest of the Philistines, contained along coast.
         b. Conquest of Aram or Syria (Kingdom of Zobah).
         c. Conquest of Moab and Ammon in Transjordan, made tributary peoples.
         d. Conquest of Edom in the south.
            (Note: David's conquests gave him control from Damascus in the north to Egypt in south-east, except for Philistine and Phoenician cities on coast; held both sides of Jordan; had access to Red Sea. Trade with Phoenicians.)
         e. Kindness to Saul's survivors (II Sam. 9).
      4. Family Affairs
         a. Affair with Bathsheba and reproval by prophet Nathan   Bathsheba
(II Sam. 11, 12).
         b. Amnon's rape of Tamar, Absalom's murder of Amnon,   Absalom
and Absalom's exile and recall (II Sam. 13, 14).
         c. Absalom's conspiracy (II Sam. 15--18).
      5. Return of David as King (II Sam. 19).
      6. Revolt of the North under Sheba the Benjamite (II Sam. 20).
      7. An appendix, out of order chronologically.
         a. David's Psalm of Thanksgiving (II Sam. 22, Psalm 19).
         b. David's sin of numbering the people (II Sam. 24).
         c. Last words of David (II Sam. 23:1-7).

David's Empire

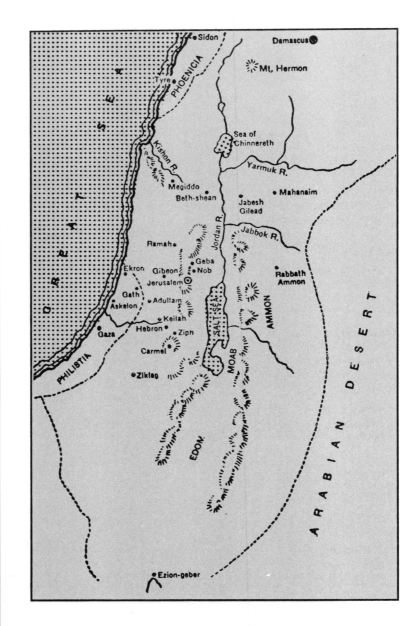

THE EMPIRE OF KING DAVID

II. PSALMS

A. Old Testament Poetry

1. Many of the first 72 psalms are attributed to David as well as some others; it is difficult to know which ones are really David's.
2. The Book of Psalms is a collection of songs and hymns written over a long period of time by many authors; collection completed about 100 B.C., a thousand years after David.
3. Most of the books of the Old Testament contain poetry. The prophets wrote almost wholly in poetry.

B. Characteristics of Hebrew Poetry

1. Use of two parallel lines to express the desired thought. The first line introduces the thought, and the second line reiterates it, adds to it or contrasts it.
2. Uses parallelism rather than meter for rhythm, and repetition rather than rhyme. The effect is one of rising and falling tone, especially useful for antiphonal and recitational uses.
3. Charm is in its earnestness, and picturesqueness, in its vivid words and phrases which express the deepest emotions and experiences of man.
4. Because Hebrew poetry does not rely on rhyme or meter, it is as beautiful in translation as in the original.
5. Certain psalms have an alphabetical succession of initial letters of lines or verse (this cannot be seen in English translation).
6. Sometimes includes a play on two similar Hebrew words; this is lost in translation.

C. Arrangement of Psalms

1. Book I - Psalms 1-41 (concluding with doxology 41:13)
   Introduction (1, 2)
   A Davidic collection (3-41)
2. Book II - Psalms 42-72 (ending with doxology 72:18-19)
   Psalms of Korah musical guild (42-49)
   Second Davidic collection (51-72)

Psalms

3. Book III - Psalms 73-89 (ending with doxology 89:52)
   Psalms of the Asaph musical guild (73-83 plus 50)
   Additional psalms of Korah guild (84-88, except 86)
4. Book IV - Psalms 90-106 (ending with doxology 106:48)
   Psalms of Yahweh's kingship (93-99, except 94)
   Songs of Praise (103-106)
5. Book V - Psalms 107-150 (concluding with doxology 150:1-6)
   Psalms of pilgrimage (120-134)
   A third Davidic collection (138-145)
   Hallelujah psalms (111-118, 146-150)
6. Classifications of some of the Psalms by content and/or type:
   Songs of Trust (11, 23, 27, 46, 62, 63, 66, 91, 121, 125, 131)
   Hymns of Praise (8, 19, 24, 29, 33, 46-48, 93, 95-101, 103-107,
   110, 111, 113, 114, 117, 135, 136, 144-150)
   Laments (entreaties) (3-7, 9, 10, 12-14, 17, 22, 25, 26, 28, 31,
   32, 35-39, 42-44, 51-61, 64-71, 74, 77, 79, 80, 83, 85, 86, 88-90,
   94, 102, 106, 109, 120, 123, 126, 129, 130, 137, 139-143)
   Thanksgiving Songs (30, 32, 40, 65, 75, 67, 92, 103, 107, 108,
   111, 116, 118, 124, 138)
   Festival Liturgies (worship) (15, 24, 46, 47, 48, 50, 68, 76, 82,
   84, 87, 115, 118, 122, 125, 132, 134)

Solomon

   Wisdom Psalms (1, 19, 37, 49, 73, 112, 119, 127, 128, 133)
   Messianic (2, 8, 16, 22, 31, 40, 41, 45, 68, 69, 102, 110, 118)
   Historical (18, 20, 21, 34, 46, 48, 72, 78, 81, 105-106, 135-137)

III. "SOLOMON IN ALL HIS GLORY"
A. The Career of Solomon, Son of David (965-926 B.C.)

1. Conspiracy of Adonijah and Joab; anointing of Solomon (I
   Kings 1).
2. Death of David (2:1-12).
3. Solomon destroys opposition: Adonijah, Joab, Shimei
   (2:13-46).
4. Solomon's prayer and reputation for wisdom (3:4-28).
5. Substitution of administrative districts for tribal organization

Temple

   to impose taxation for elaborate court and military
   establishment (I Kings 4).
6. Building of the Temple, and other elaborate palaces and
   buildings (I Kings 5--7).
7. Dedication of the Temple built to house the Tabernacle of
   Moses [Tent of Meeting] about 960 B.C. (I Kings 8).
8. Foreign alliances, trade (I Kings 9).
9. Visit of Queen of Sheba (Ethiopia or southern Arabia) (I
   Kings 10).
10. Worldliness, idolatry, and dissension (I Kings 11).
11. Revolt of the northern tribes after death of Solomon (I Kings
    12), c. 926 B.C..

IV. PROVERBS, SONG OF SOLOMON, ECCLESIASTES
A. Authorship
1. Three books traditionally attributed to Solomon who was known as a composer of proverbs and songs (I Kings 4:32), but with the exception perhaps of some of the proverbs, Solomon's authorship is unlikely.

B. Proverbs (seven collections of sayings dated 350-150 B.C.)
Proverbs
1. Praise of wisdom attributed to Solomon (Prov. 1--9).
2. Collection of sayings attributed to Solomon (10:1--22:16).
3. Simple truths stated, almost identical with an Egyptian wisdom book of 1000-600 B.C. (22:17--24:34).
4. A collection of wise sayings attributed to Solomon (Prov. 25--29).
5. The words of Agur (Prov. 30).
6. The words of Lemuel (31:1-9).
7. Tribute to Woman (31:10-31).

C. Song of Solomon (usually dated about 300 B.C. -- 600 years after Solomon)
Song of Solomon
1. A love song or a collection of wedding songs considered as an allegory by the Jews with "the beloved" as Jehovah and "the bride" as Israel.
2. Christians took the allegory to mean the love of Christ for the Church.

D. Ecclesiastes (usually dated around 200 B.C.)
Ecclesiastes
1. A collection of discourses, observations, and wise sayings on the vanity (emptiness) of human life without God.

V. THE DIVIDED KINGDOM (Kings and Prophets) c. 926-721 B.C.
A. Prophets
Prophets
1. One who speaks for God (not necessarily one who foretells the future).
2. Failure to heed warnings would bring on calamities foretold.
3. Prophets usually had both a social message and a religious message.
4. Prophets emerged in times of crisis.
5. Common messages of the prophets:
   Prophetic Messages
   a. Declared Yahweh as the one Lord over all peoples.
   b. Denounced worship of false gods.
   c. Denounced animal sacrifice, fasting, feasting, ritual observance.
   d. Denounced breaking of the laws of the Covenant, especially social obligations to the poor, the widow, and the orphan.
   e. Interpreted Israel's enemies as punishment for Israel's sins; sin brings its own punishment.
   f. Declared Day of the Lord (Or Day of Judgement, which would begin the reign of God) was soon, not afar off.

g. Declared a remnant would endure and form the basis for a new Israel.

h. Expectation of a Messiah, an "anointed one", a deliverer.

6. Prophet's messages by means of poetic images and metaphors.

B. Important Kings and Prophets of the Two Kingdoms

Kingdom of Judah (South) (also portion of Benjamin, and a number of Levites)	Kingdom of Israel (North) (also called Samaria or Ephraim --10 tribes)
<div align="center">**c. 926 B.C.**</div>	
<div align="center">**Tenth Century**</div>	
King Rehoboam (Solomon's son) (I Kings 12:1-24) **"J" Document originates** **King Asa** (I Kings 15; II Chron. 14--16)	**King Jeroboam** (foreman of forced labor under Solomon; sets up calf gods and shrines at Bethel and Dan) (I Kings 12:25-33)
<div align="center">**Ninth Century**</div>	
King Jehoshaphat (I Kings 22; II Kings 3; II Chron. 17--20)	**King Omri** (Samaria made capitol) (I Kings 16: 23-27) **Prophet Elijah (Elias)** - time of King Ahab and Jezebel and Tyrian Baal worship -Elijah and the widow at Zarephath (multiplies food; restores child) (I Kings 17) -Elijah's challenge to Baal prophets (I Kings 18) -Flees from Jezebel to Horeb where he hears the still small voice (I Kings 19) -Rebukes the taking of Na- both's vineyard (I Kings 21) -Ascension (II Kings 2:1-11)
[In the course of its more than 300 years as a kingdom, Judah had 20 kings, all descendents of David. In its shorter 200 years as a kingdom, Israel had 19 kings with successive ruling families overthrown by coups.]	**Prophet Elisha** (pupil of Elijah) -Elisha succeeds Elijah (II Kings 2:12-25) -Multiplies food, heals woman of sterility, restores child, neutralizes pottage (II Kings 4) -Heals Naaman of leprosy (II Kings 5) -Elisha adviser to four kings (II Kings 6--10; 13)

Divided Kingdom

Rehoboam
Jeroboam

J Document

Asa

Jehoshaphat
Omri

Ahab
Jezebel

Elijah

Elisha

Judah (continued)	Israel (continued)	

Eighth Century

Judah	Israel	
Prophet Micah (in villages) -Judgment for sin (Micah 1--3) -Promise of peace and the Messiah (Micah 4--5) -"What doth the Lord require" (Micah 6--7) **Prophet Isaiah** (and **King Hezekiah**) -Call (Isa. 6, 7, 8) -Adviser to Kings (Isa. 1:1) -Adviser to King Hezekiah (II Kings 18, 19) -Reformation under King Hezekiah (II Chron. 29--31) -Judah doesn't fall to Assyria (II Kings 19; Isa. 36, 37) -Healing of Hezekiah (II Kings 20:1-11; Isa. 38) -Foretells Fall of Judah to Babylon (Isa. 39)	"E" Document originates **Prophet Amos** -Judgments against the nations (Amos 1--2) -Judgments on unrepentant, unjust Israel (Amos 3--6) -Series of visions (7:1-9:10) -Restored Israel (9:11-15) **Prophet Hosea** -The prophet and his unfaithful wife; a lesson (Hosea 1--3) -The message: the unchanging love of God (Hosea 4--14) **Fall of Samaria to Assyria,** 721 B. C. (II Kings 17); end of the kingdom of Israel; dispersal of inhabitants	E Document Micah Amos Isaiah Hosea Hezekiah Fall of Israel to Assyria

C. **Poems of Isaiah**
1. Need for repentance and restoration (Isa. 1--5).
2. Coming reign of Messiah (Isa. 9:1--10:4; 11:1--12:6).
3. Judgments against the nations (Isa. 10:5-34; 13:1--23:18).
4. The coming Day of the Lord--the Lord's kingdom (Isa. 24--27).
5. Folly of dependence on nations (Isa. 28--32).
6. Judgment on Edom; redemption of Zion (Isa. 33--35).

D. **Prophet Joel** (date uncertain, may be 8th century, possibly as late as 400 B.C.
1. The plague of locusts and a plea of repentance (Joel 1:1--2:17).
2. Promise of reward for penitence (2:18--3:21).

E. **Story of Jonah** (date uncertain; about a prophet of the eighth century, probably written about 350 B.C.)
1. Jonah's commission, his flight and punishment (Jonah 1).
2. His prayer of deliverance (Jonah 2).
3. His obedience to his charge and Nineveh's repentance (Jonah 3).
4. His displeasure and the divine rebuke to him (Jonah 4).

(margin notes: Isaiah; Joel; Jonah)

VI. THE KINGDOM OF JUDAH (about 721-586 B.C.)

Josiah

A. King Josiah (640-609 B.C.)

1. Boy king, eight years old when reign began; great grandson of King Hezekiah.

D Document

2. Religious reforms: finding of book of Deuteronomy; abolition of high places, idols, and foreign religious practices; insistence on a single central shrine in Jerusalem for sacrificial worship (II Kings 22, 23; II Chron. 34, 35).

3. Three prophets during his reign: Zephaniah, Nahum, and Jeremiah, and possibly also Habakkuk.

Zephaniah

B. Prophet Zephaniah

1. The Day of the Lord is come and judgment on Judah (Zeph. 1--3).

Nahum

C. Prophet Nahum

1. Prediction of and exaltation over the coming downfall of Assyria (Nineveh) (Nahum 1--3).

Habakkuk

D. Prophet Habakkuk (possibly during reign of Jehoiakim, son of Josiah)

1. God is "of purer eyes than to behold evil" and "the just shall live by his faith" (Hab. 1--3).

Jeremiah

E. Prophet Jeremiah (during reigns of Josiah, Jehoahaz, Jehoiakim and Zedekiah--42 years)

1. Before the fall of Judah.

    a. Birthplace and call (626 B.C.) (Jer. 1; 7:1-7).

    b. Never married (Jer. 16:1-9).

    c. Opposition from family and others (11:1--12:6).

    d. Opposition of other prophets (Jer. 26--28).

    e. Makes example of Rechabites (Jer. 35).

    f. King Jehoiakim had Jeremiah's writings burned (Jer. 36).

    g. Jeremiah placed in stocks (20:1-6).

2. After first captivity, 598 B.C.

    a. Letter to early captives in Babylon (Jer. 29).

    b. Advice to King Zedekiah during siege (Jer. 21; 34).

    c. Prisoner in Zedekiah's court (Jer. 37; 38).

    d. Cast into dungeon and released by Ethiopian (38:4-13).

    e. Ethiopian's reward (39:15-18).

3. After destruction of Jerusalem, 586 B.C.

    a. Purchase of land (Jer. 32).

    b. Protected by Nebuchadnezzar (Jer. 39).

    c. Released from among captives and allowed to remain in Judah (Jer. 40).

    d. Fled to Egypt and continued preaching (Jer. 42--44).

F. Parallels Between Life of Jeremiah and Life of Jesus

1. Both often alone and both drank deeply of prayer.

2. Both rejected by their kin and townsmen.

3. Both renounced the religious figures of their times.
4. Both wept over the coming woes to Jerusalem.
5. Both denounced vain trust in the Temple.
6. Jeremiah foresaw the New Testament (Covenant) which Jesus fulfilled.

G. The Message of Jeremiah (sermons dictated to Baruch who incorporated biographical material along with them)

1. Certain warnings to Judah (Jer. 2--6).
2. Unacceptable worship (Jer. 7).
3. Results of blindness to sin (Jer. 8--10).
4. Appeal for repentance (12:7--15:9).
5. Warnings by word and symbol of potter (16:10--19:14).
6. Prophecy of capture of Israel by Babylon (Jer. 22--25). [Note: Messianic King 23:5, 6; vision of the figs 24:1-11].
7. The promise of restoration and a New Covenant (Jer. 30--33) [Note: New Covenant 31:31-34].
8. Against foreign nations (Jer. 46--52).

H. Fall of Jerusalem to Babylon, 598 B.C. and End of Kingdom of Judah, 586 B.C. (II Kings 24:18--25:30; Jer. 52).

1. Invasion by Nebuchadnezzar, king of Babylonian Empire and capture of Jerusalem, 598 B.C.; king of Judah and some 10,000 Jews taken captive including Ezekiel.
2. Siege of Jerusalem and fall of the city, 586 B.C. and forced exile of peoples; Temple destroyed.

I. Lamentations

1. Traditionally ascribed to Jeremiah, but most likely not by him.
2. A lament or dirge over the fall of Jerusalem.

J. Succession of Empires

1. Israel population dispersed by Assyria (721 B.C.); Judah made vassal of Assyria.
2. Judah to become a province of successive empires: Babylon 586-538, Persia 538-332, Greece 332-168 B.C.

Jeremiah

Fall of Judah to Babylon

Lamentations

Babylonian Figures

Empires

Obadiah

    K. Prophet Obadiah (dating very uncertain, may be as late as 400 B.C. or as early as the 6th century)
        1. A denunciation of Edom, ancient enemy of Judah.
        2. Message: The Day of the Lord is coming.

Exile
Captivity in
Babylon

Ezekiel

VII. THE EXILE--CAPTIVITY OF JUDAH IN BABYLON (6th Century, about 586-538 B.C.)
    A. Ezekiel, Prophet of the Captivity
        1. Began work in Judah (perhaps as a student of Jeremiah); taken to Babylon and allowed to continue work (Ezek. 1:1-3; 3:15-24).
        2. Message.
            a. Call to prophesy in an apocalyptic vision of the glory, holiness, and majesty of God (Ezek. 1--3).
            b. Warnings to Jerusalem prior to siege and destruction (Ezek. 4--24).
            c. Condemnation of hostile nations (Ezek. 25--32; 35).
            d. Individual responsibility for repentance (Ezek. 18).
            e. Ezekiel, a watchman (Ezek. 33).
            f. God as a shepherd will lead and protect (Ezek. 34).
            g. Israel shall be restored, resurrection of "dry bones," and Gog and Magog destroyed (Ezek. 36--39).
            h. The New Jerusalem and the New Temple (Ezek. 40--48).

Deutero-Isaiah

    B. The Second Isaiah (or Deutero-Isaiah)
        1. Prophet of the Captivity in Babylon (Isa. 40--66); some scholars ascribe chapters 56 to 66 to a somewhat later Third Isaiah writing in Jerusalem).
        2. Nothing beyond his writing is known of this great prophet-poet-theologian of the sixth century.
        3. Message.
            a. The Comforter (Isa. 40).
            b. God will restore Israel (Isa. 41).
            c. Israel, the Servant of the Lord (42:1--44:23)
            d. Cyrus appointed to restore Israel (44:24--48:22).
            e. Mission of the Servant of the Lord (49:1--51:16).
            f. Awake (51:17--52:12).
            g. Messiah (52:13--53:12).
            h. The Woman--New Jerusalem (Isa. 54, 55).
            i. Sins delay complete restoration (Isa. 56--59).
            j. Glory of the New Jerusalem and the destruction of evil (Isa. 60--66).

C. Daniel, Hananiah (Shadrach), Mishael (Meshach), Azariah (Abednego)
   1. Hebrew boys reared in King Nebuchadnezzar's palace; refused to eat the king's food and drink (Dan. 1).
   2. Daniel interprets Nebuchadnezzar's dream of a monstrous idol of iron, clay, brass, silver, and gold which falls apart when struck by "a stone cut without hands" (Dan. 2).
   3. Shadrach, Meshach, and Abednego in fiery furnace (Dan. 3).
   4. Nebuchadnezzar's madness (Dan. 4).
   5. Daniel interprets writing on wall at Belshazzar's feast (Dan. 5).
D. Fall of Babylonian Empire to Persia (538 B.C.)
   1. Exiles allowed to return to Judea by King Cyrus of Persia.
E. The Chronicles (written late, sometime after 500 B.C.)
   1. A glamorized, idealized re-writing of the history of the Jews, written at least two centuries later than the books of Samuel and Kings.
   2. Written from a priestly point of view as an introduction to the books of Ezra and Nehemiah with attention fixed on the Temple, and the glory of the Kingdom of Judah; omits material that would challenge its thesis.
   3. Contents.
       a. Genealogical tables to the death of Saul (I Chron. 1--10).
       b. Reign of David and accession of Solomon (I Chron. 11--29).
       c. Reign of Solomon (II Chron. 1--9).
       d. From Rehoboam to Jehoshaphat (II Chron. 10--20).
       e. From Jehoram to Hezekiah (II Chron. 21--28).
       f. From Hezekiah to the Exile and Restoration (II Chron. 29--36).

VIII. CONTEMPORARY THINKERS OF THE 6TH CENTURY B.C.
   A. Contemporaries of Jeremiah, Ezekiel, II Isaiah
   1. Zoroaster (630-553) in Persia.
   2. Buddha (550-480) in India.
   3. Confucius (551-479) in China.
   4. Lao-tse (b. 604) in China.
   5. Solon (640-560) in Greece (Athenian laws).

Daniel
Hananiah
Mishael
Azariah

Fall of Babylon
to Persia

Chronicles

Contemporary
Leaders

FROM DANIEL TO CHRIST JESUS

(circa 500 B.C. to 0)

"Behold, I will send my messenger, and he shall prepare the way before me: and the Lord, whom ye seek, shall suddenly come to his temple, even the messenger of the covenant."   -Malachi 3:1

I. THE RETURN AND PERSIAN PERIOD (538-332 B.C.)

Daniel

    A. Daniel

        1. Daniel made one of three presidents over 120 princes of Babylonia by Persian king (Dan. 5:31; 6:1).

        2. Daniel thrown into den of lions (Dan. 6).

Zerubbabel

    B. Zerubbabel

        1. First group returns led by Sheshbazzar (commissioned by Persian King Cyrus) (Ezra 1).

        2. Second group returns (under Darius I) led by Zerubbabel (Neh. 7).

Temple

        3. Zerubbabel rebuilds Jerusalem and lays foundation for new Temple on old Temple site (Ezra 3--6).

        4. Temple completed about 515 B.C.

    C. Prophets During the Rebuilding (Ezra 5:1)

Haggai

        1. **Haggai**.

            a. Urging restoration of the Temple (Haggai 1).

            b. Encouraging workers to go forward (Haggai 2).

Zechariah

        2. **Zechariah** (apocalyptic--almost all by vision and symbol).

            a. Visions present a picture of a restored Jerusalem in which prosperity, purity, and harmony dwell; the nations that molest it will themselves be destroyed.

            b. Eight visions of Zechariah (Zech. 1--6).

            c. Fasts and feasts and the coming glory of Jerusalem (Zech. 7, 8).

            d. Additions by other and later prophets:

                (1) Kingdom established and heathen overthrown (Zech. 9--11).

                (2) Another apocalypse (Zech. 12--14).

Ezra

    D. Ezra, Priest and Scribe

        1. Comes from Babylon about 60 years after Temple is completed with large group of exiles (Ezra 7:1-26) with letter from Persian King Artaxerxes II naming him religious leader of the community.

2. Establishes Jewish hierarchy conceived by Ezekiel and proclaims priestly law (Ezra sometimes has been called the second Moses). Priestly laws incorporated into Leviticus, Numbers and Exodus along with Mosaic laws of 1,000 years before. Writing of "P" Document, including Gen. 1:1--2:3, perhaps as an introduction to Torah. Torah reedited to substantially its present form; I and II Chronicles written.

Ezra

P Document

3. Dissolves foreign marriages of exiles (Ezra 9; 10).
4. Beginning of the high priests as the rulers in religious matters.
5. Ruth and Jonah written as protests against narrowness of Ezra.

Ruth
Jonah
Nehemiah

E. Nehemiah, Governor of Jerusalem and Builder of the Wall
   1. Persian king appoints Nehemiah governor and allows him to direct rebuilding of the wall of Jerusalem. In 52 days, despite opposition, the job is finished (Neh. 1:1--7:4).
   2. Dedication of walls (12:27-43).
   3. Reading of the Law to the people (Neh. 8).
   4. Dedication of people to Law (Neh. 9; 10; 13:1-3).
   5. One out of ten chosen by lot to dwell in Jerusalem (11:1-2).
   6. Reforms of Nehemiah (13:4-31).

II. ESTHER, JEWESS MARRIED TO A PERSIAN KING
   A. The Book of Esther
   1. Story set in the 5th century, but written around 150 B.C.
   2. Story of a Jewess, Queen of Persia, who risked her life to save her people from danger.
   3. Book is read by the Jews at the Feast of Purim (in March).
   4. Book is patriotic; does not mention name of God.

Esther

III. MALACHI
   A. Last of the Prophets
   1. Written in the latter part of the 5th century B.C.; author's name is not known; Malachi means "messenger" in Hebrew.
   2. Message.
      a. Israel has profaned God (Mal. 1, 2).
      b. The way of redemption (Mal. 3, 4).

Malachi

IV. OLD TESTAMENT COMPLETE
   A. Hebrew Scriptures
   1. By the latter part of the fourth century B.C., the Hebrew scriptures were virtually completed.
   2. Actual canonization did not occur until about 400 B.C. for the Law [Torah]; 200 B.C. for the Prophets; and not until A.D. 90 for the Writings by Jewish Council at Jamnia.
   3. Last books to be accorded inspired status included Jonah, Ruth, Esther, Daniel, and Job.

Old Testament

V. GREEK PERIOD (332-168 B.C.)

    A. The Greek "Golden Age" -- 5th Century

        1. Athens, the seat of learning; Socrates (470-399) and his student, Plato (427-347), and Plato's student, Aristotle (384-322); Aristotle's student, Alexander the Great (356-323), extended Hellenistic culture and power throughout most of the civilized world.

Fall of Persia
to Greece

    B. The Persian Empire Conquered by Alexander the Great (332 B.C.)

Hellenistic
Culture

        1. Greeks brought man-centered view of life, a new world language, athletics and stadia, theatre and drama, music, art, civic life (with a typical Greek city in every area).

        2. The city of Alexandria in Egypt became a world center of Greek culture and learning.

        3. Death of Alexander (323 B.C.).

    C. Empire Divided Among Greek Generals

        1. Syria went to Seleucus and Egypt to Ptolemy.

        2. Palestine becomes pawn between rival Seleucids and Ptolemies; first annexed to Egypt, then to Syria.

VI. GREEK INFLUENCE

    A. Wisdom Literature

Job
Proverbs
Ecclesiastes

        1. A response of the Jews to Hellenistic culture and learning

        2. Canonical Wisdom writings include Job, Proverbs, and Ecclesiastes.

        3. Apocryphal Wisdom writings include the <u>Wisdom of Solomon</u>, and <u>Ecclesiasticus</u> (also called <u>Sirach</u>).

Wisdom Literature

    B. Nature of Wisdom literature

        1. "Wisdom" considered in three ways.

            a. Wisdom as Creative Mind or Principle.

            b. Wisdom as the right way of living (human goodness, morality, understanding, religion).

            c. Wisdom as the expedient way to conduct one's life for there is material gain for virtuous living.

Psalms

    C. Psalms

        1. Collection of Psalms, an anthology of songs and hymns probably completed during this period.

        2. About one-third of Psalms written during this time.

VII. OLD TESTAMENT TRANSLATED INTO GREEK (285 B.C.)

Septuagint

    A. Septuagint (sometimes called LXX)

        1. Greek translation by Jewish scholars in Alexandria.

        2. Septuagint became Scriptures of all Greek-speaking Jews, later also of Greek-speaking Christians.

        3. Septuagint included apocryphal books later rejected for the Hebrew Bible at the Council of Jamnia (A.D. 90).

VIII. MACCABEAN PERIOD (168-63 B.C.)

A. Maccabean Revolt

1. Judea came under Seleucid control in 198 B.C.
2. An effort of the Seleucid (Syrian) king, Antiochus IV, to stamp out Judaism brought on the Maccabean revolt about 169 B.C. (See I Maccabees in Apocrypha).
3. In 166, when leader of revolt, Mattathias, died, his son, Judas Maccabeus took control; in December, 165, Temple rededicated (commemoration of that event is called the Feast of Dedication, Festival of Lights, or Hanukkah).
4. Eighty year period of independence under the Maccabees (143-63 B.C.).

Maccabean Independence

B. Literature

1. Books of **Daniel** and **Esther** belong to this period, both accounts of earlier heroes whose lives and deeds would encourage the Jews to stand fast against tyranny.

Esther

2. The Apocalypse of **Daniel** (Dan. 7--12).

Daniel

   a. Virtually all modern scholars contend that Daniel is not a book of "prophecy" looking forward from the Babylonian period to 168 B.C., but a book written in 168 looking back to the Babylonian period to provide encouragement in present persecution.
   b. Apocalyptic writing, vision or dream literature, symbolic pictures, making Daniel the best example of this type of writing in the Old Testament. The New Testament apocalypse, Revelation, quotes from Daniel 50 times.

IX. APOCRYPHA AND THE DEAD SEA SCROLLS

A. Apocrypha (c. 190-50 B.C.)

1. Apocryphal writings in Greek include Ecclesiasticus, I, II Maccabees, Judith, Tobit, Wisdom of Solomon, I, II Esdras, Additions to Esther, Baruch, Prayer of Manasseh, Song of the Three Holy Children, History of Susanna, and Bel and the Dragon, the latter three additions to Daniel. Provide insight into religious thinking of this period.

Apocrypha

B. Dead Sea Scrolls (c. 150 B.C.--A.D. 68)

1. Discovered in 1947 by shepherds in cave near the northern shore of Dead Sea; further finds since that time.
2. Thousands of scroll fragments, including all Old Testament books (except Esther), commentaries, apocryphal and pseudepigraphical books and sectarian documents.
3. Essene documents like the Manual of Discipline and The War of the Sons of Light with the Sons of Darkness scroll show the Qumran community awaiting the kingdom of God.
4. Important in understanding the historical and cultural situation in which Jesus appeared.

Dead Sea Scrolls

eight

<table>
<tr><td>Fall of Judea
to Rome</td><td>

X. ROME RULES THE WORLD
  A. Judea Falls to Pompey in 63 B.C.
    1. Herod named by the Romans as king of province of Judea (reigned 40 B.C. to 4 B.C.).
    2. Roman empire was one enormous unit held together by one political ruler; one language (Greek); one imperial cult (emperor worship); and by roads, bridges, and commerce.
    3. Empire itself established by Augustus Caesar, first emperor (27 B.C. to A.D. 14).

XI. JUDAISM AT THE END OF THE FIRST CENTURY, B.C.
  A. Sects of Judaism

</td></tr>
</table>

X. ROME RULES THE WORLD

Fall of Judea to Rome

  A. Judea Falls to Pompey in 63 B.C.

    1. Herod named by the Romans as king of province of Judea (reigned 40 B.C. to 4 B.C.).

    2. Roman empire was one enormous unit held together by one political ruler; one language (Greek); one imperial cult (emperor worship); and by roads, bridges, and commerce.

    3. Empire itself established by Augustus Caesar, first emperor (27 B.C. to A.D. 14).

XI. JUDAISM AT THE END OF THE FIRST CENTURY, B.C.

  A. Sects of Judaism

Pharisees

    1. Pharisees.

      a. Resisted Hellenizing; primarily townspeople, scholars, teachers, professional people.

      b. Characterized by religious devotion; absolute observance of Law; emphasis on Torah; religion of the synagogue though they went to the Temple on feast days.

      c. Introduced new ideas of resurrection, last judgment, punishment after death.

Sadducees

    2. Sadducees.

      a. Compromised with Greeks and Romans; primarily members of the aristocratic priesthood and the well-to-do.

      b. Religiously extremely conservative; religion of the Temple and sacrificial worship.

      c. Did not accept resurrection or judgment.

Essenes

    3. Essenes.

      a. Monastic community life with emphasis on discipline (discipleship).

      b. Emphasis on baptism, purification.

      c. Followed a "Teacher of Righteousness".

      d. Large collection of books (Dead Sea Scrolls were Essene library).

      e. Taught that the judgment was near.

      f. John the Baptist may have been an Essene.

Zealots

    4. Zealots.

      a. Revolutionaries, sought to overthrow the government and drive out the Romans.

      b. Revolutionary activity of this group led to destruction of Jerusalem A.D. 70.

    5. Common People.

      a. Participated in synagogue services and Temple feasts but did not identify with any sect.

      b. The crowds that sought Jesus were mostly from this group.

c. Extremely poor, struggled for a bare hand-to-mouth existence.

B. Temple Services

1. Daily.

    a. Forenoon and afternoon--sacrifice and incense, formal prayers and musical liturgy.

2. Special services and private sacrifice throughout the day.

C. Chief Celebrations

1. Passover (Ex. 12:1-30; Lev. 23:4-14; Deut. 16:1-8).

    a. Feast of unleavened bread commemorating deliverance from Egypt.

    b. Week-long celebration in March or April.

2. Pentecost (Lev. 23:15-22; Deut. 16:9-12).

    a. Feast of weeks commemorating Moses' proclamation of the law from Mt. Sinai.

    b. Fifty days after the Passover in June.

3. Day of Atonement (Lev. 16:1-34; 23:26-32).

    a. "The Day." A fast and ceremonial.

    b. September or October (Yom Kippur).

4. Tabernacles (Lev. 23:33-44; Deut. 16:13-15).

    a. A feast commemorating the wilderness journey, similar to our Thanksgiving Day with feasting and good cheer.

    b. September or October (Sukkoth).

5. Feast of Dedication (I Macc. 4:52-59; II Macc. 10:5-8)

    a. A feast commemorating Maccabean restoration and rededication of the Temple; also called "Festival of Lights".

    b. December (Hanukkah).

D. Scribes (scholars, doctors of the Law, lawyers)

1. Copied, studied, interpreted and taught the Law.

E. Sanhedrin (Temple Council)

1. Supreme court of appeal for the Jews in religious matters.

2. Seventy-one Sadducees and Pharisees with the High Priest presiding.

F. The Synagogue

1. Synagogue School from ages 5 or 6 to 13; Bible was the only textbook. Study was first of the Law, then the Prophets, and finally the Writings.

2. Building was for religious instruction and worship; also served as a courthouse, school, reading room, and parish house--a community center.

3. Ten males could organize a synagogue; governed by elected elders; autonomous and independent of other synagogues (nearly 500 synagogues said to have been in Jerusalem alone).

4. Platform and reader's desk from which the Law was read and interpreted.

[margin notes: Temple Services; Jewish Feasts; Scribes; Sanhedrin; Synagogue]

Synagogue
Services

5. Services (see Luke 4:16-30).
 a. Recital of Shema (Deut. 6:4-9).
 b. Responsive readings--Prayer and "Amen".
 c. Reading of "Law," then "Prophets" in Hebrew followed by interpretation in Aramaic or Greek.
 d. Singing of Psalms.

Temple

G. Herod's Temple
1. The Temple was rebuilt and enlarged by Herod the Great. Begun in 20 B.C. and finished only shortly before its destruction in A.D. 70.
2. This was the third Temple. The first was built by Solomon about 1,000 B.C. and destroyed by Nebuchadnezzar. The second was built by Zerubbabel about 500 B.C. and desolated as a result of revolts.
3. Plan of Herod's Temple (elaborate courts surrounding the Temple itself).
 a. Royal Porch--rabbinical schools.
 b. Solomon's Porch--religious propaganda meetings.
 c. Court of Gentiles--where birds and animals were offered for sale.
 d. Court of Women (and laity)--where Jesus taught and healed.
 e. Court of Israel--accessible only to Jewish male worshippers.
 f. Court of Priests for Levite activities--containing brazen altar and laver where priests and laymen participated in ritualistic sacrifices of animals.
 g. The Temple itself.
  (1) Holy Place--for priests (contained the seven-branched golden candlestick, table of shewbread and altar of incense).
  (2) Curtains--veil.
  (3) Most Holy Place or "Holy of Holies"--which highpriest only could enter on Day of Atonement (in Herod's Temple it was absolutely empty).

H. Important Ages

Age 12

1. On completing his twelfth or during his thirteenth year, the Jewish boy was eligible for Bar Mitzvah, a ceremony recognizing his reaching the age of responsibility and religious duty.

Age 20

2. On reaching the age of twenty, the Jewish young man was granted full religious citizenship.

CHRIST JESUS

(circa 7 B.C. to A.D. 30)

"And the Word was made flesh, and dwelt among us, . . . For the law was given by Moses, but grace and truth came by Jesus Christ." -John 1:14, 17

I. DEVELOPMENT OF THE CONCEPT OF THE CHRIST
  A. Some Allusions in Early Writings
    1. Spirit of God (Gen. 1:2).
    2. The seed of the woman (Gen. 3:15).
    3. Visit of the three (Gen. 18).
    4. Angel before thee (Ex. 23:20-26).
    5. A prophet like Moses (Deut. 18:15).
    6. Melchizedek (Gen. 14:18-20; see also Psalm 110; Heb. 5--9; Rev. 1:6).
  B. The Anointed One (Hebrew: Mashiah or Messiah [Greek: Messias]. Greek equivalent: Christos or Christ)
    1. Messiah occurs only twice in the Old Testament (Dan. 9:25, 26) but its Hebrew equivalent "Mashiah" (Mashiach) occurs some 38 times and in some cases is translated literally "anointed."
    2. Anointing with oil: kings and priests anointed literally; prophets anointed metaphorically (Isa. 61:1-3).
  C. Some Passages in the Old Testament Regarded as Messianic
    1. Immanuel or "God-with-us" (Isa. 7:14).
    2. King (Isa. 9:2-7; 11:2-10; Psalms 2).
    3. Son of Man (Dan. 7:13, 14).
    4. Everlasting Light (Isa. 60:19).
    5. Shepherd (Ezek. 34:23, 24; 37:24, 25).
    6. Savior and Deliverer (Zech. 9--14).
    7. Of the House of David (Gen. 49:8-10; Num. 24:17-19; Micah 5:2-4; Isa. 11:1; Jer. 23:5, 6; Hos. 3:5).
    8. Suffering Servant (Isa. 52:13--53:12).
    9. A Light to the Gentiles (Isa. 49:6; 42:6, 7).
    10. Messenger (Isa. 52:7-12; Malachi 3, 4).
  D. Greek Influence: Erhomenos (the One who is coming)
    1. The Logos, universal Reason that would come to dwell with all men.
    2. Logos also identified with "Nous" (Mind), "idea of good" or divine revelation.
    3. Logos or Word in Hebrew literature also identified with Wisdom (Ps. 33:6; 107:20; 119; see also John 1:1-18).

Allusions

Anointed

Messiah

Logos

49

E. Christology: What is the Nature of the Christ?

Christ

    1. Christ, the idea of God, expressing the nature of God, Spirit, divine reality. Jesus taught that God is the ultimate reality, both present and to come, a clear, living, present reality, good, and expressed in a good life and moral attitude whereby the "pure in heart" perceive God.

    2. Christ, the idea of sonship, expressing the nature of man as the image and likeness of God. Jesus called himself the Son of God as well as the son of man; he taught man's sonship and continuing relationship with the Father.

    3. Christ, the idea of redemption, expressing the nature of God's activity in the world. Jesus taught a loving Father who seeks to welcome repentant sons in love--redeems them: He promised the Paraclete "Comforter" [Advocate, Defender, Helper, Strengthener, the Spirit of Truth--the Holy Ghost or Holy Spirit] which would bring salvation, grace, healing, reconciliation, transformation, new birth.

    4. Christ, the title of Jesus. Jesus was regarded by the disciples as "the anointed One"--the Messiah or Christ. Jesus denied that he himself was God; he taught his oneness with God and the oneness of all men with the Father. Early Christians thought of Jesus as "lord" in the sense of "master"; it was later that Christians came to think of Jesus as divinity itself, to whom worship could be offered--as "Lord."

Kingdom

F. Eschatology "last things": When Will the Kingdom (reign, rule) of God Come?

    1. Realized eschatology--Reality--"Thy Kingdom come". Jesus taught that the Kingdom is already present, has arrived, but needs to be recognized or realized--an existing reality awaiting our acceptance and acknowledgment (Luke 17:20-21; 13:18-21; Matt. 12:28; 13:31-33; Mark 1:15; 4:26-32; 9:1).

    2. Apocalyptic eschatology--Kingdom coming. Parousia (presence). Jesus taught that the coming Christ-presence would be seen and felt in glory and power and usher in the Kingdom of God, establishing the Kingdom and destroying all evil. This was the expected Day of Judgment or Day of the Lord ushering in a spiritual age. Jesus taught its imminence (Mark 13:1-37; Matt. 24:1--25:46; Luke 17:22-37; 21:5-36).

Gospels

II. THE FOUR GOSPELS ("Good News")--THE BIOGRAPHIES OF JESUS

"Sayings of Jesus"

    A. Quelle meaning "source"

        1. Assumed "Sayings of Jesus" in Aramaic, now lost.

        2. Referred to by Papias, A.D. 140.

        3. Probably used by Matthew and Luke.

B. Synoptic Gospels (Mark, Matthew, Luke) Synoptics
  1. Three-sevenths of the material is common to all three
     synoptic Gospels although with variations.
  2. Mark, Matthew and Luke follow same general chronology: [1]
     Beginnings; [2] Ministry in Galilee; [3] Journey to Jerusalem;
     [4] Ministry in Judea; [5] Crucifixion-Resurrection.

C. Gospel of Mark Mark
  1. Earliest Gospel. Dated around A.D. 65 or 70 or earlier.
  2. Credited to Mark, who according to tradition, accompanied
     Peter to Rome as his interpreter (I Peter 5:13). Written for
     the Greek-speaking world. John Mark was the son of Mary
     mentioned in Acts 12:12 and is mentioned as a companion of
     Paul and Barnabas (Acts 12:25; 13:13; 15:36-39).
  3. Shortest of the Gospels. Reports primarily works rather than
     words of Jesus. Emphasis on Jesus' example.
  4. Mark 16:9-20 not in some early manuscripts.

D. Gospel of Matthew Matthew
  1. Dated around A.D. 70 or 80 or somewhat earlier.
  2. Credited wholly or in part to Matthew the disciple, a Jew.
     Relates Jesus' ministry to Old Testament prophecy.
     Emphasis on teachings, works and Messiahship.
  3. Contains about 15/16 of Mark; also "Sayings of Jesus".
  4. Contains several collections of Jesus' teachings: [1] Sermon
     on the Mount (Matt. 5--7); [2] Instructions to Disciples (Matt.
     10); [3] The Kingdom of Heaven (Matt. 13); [4] Expressing
     Christliness (Matt. 18); [5] Discourses in the Temple (Matt.
     21--23); [6] Little Apocalypse (Matt. 24--25).

E. Gospel of Luke Luke
  1. Dated around A.D. 75 or 85 or somewhat earlier.
  2. Written by the Greek physician Luke, who also wrote Acts as
     a companion book. Luke joined Paul early in his ministry
     (Acts 21:15-18) and remained with him (Col. 4:14; Philemon
     1:24; II Tim. 4:11) Both books dedicated to Theophilus,
     possibly a Roman official. Luke used Mark as a source, also
     "Sayings of Jesus".
  3. Addressed to skeptical Greek thought--emphasizes the
     Gospel message is for Gentiles as well as Jews. Dates major
     events by reference to Roman rulers. Emphasizes the
     universality of Christian Gospel, God's forgiveness, and Jesus'
     love and advocacy for poor, women, sinners, oppressed.
  4. Called "the most beautiful book ever written".

F. Gospel of John John
  1. Dated around A.D. 90 or somewhat earlier.
  2. Attributed to the disciple John. Tradition says John remained
     in Jerusalem and cared for Jesus' mother. Paul met him
     there on his third visit (Gal. 2:9). Later moved to Ephesus.

John

3. Outline of John: [1] Prologue: "Word Made Flesh" (1:1-18); [2] "Lamb of God" (1:19-51); [3] Seven Signs: "The Hour is Coming" (2:1--11:57); [4] "The Hour is Come" (12:1--13:38); [5] "The Comforter" (14:1--17:16); [6] Crucifixion and Resurrection "Lamb's Glory" (18:1--20:29); [7] Epilogue: "Witness" (20:30--21:25).

4. John brings us closest to the inner thoughts of Jesus. John's themes of life, light, love, truth, and Christ Jesus' oneness with the Father show how Jesus accomplished his works. His book is called the "metaphysical" or "spiritual" Gospel. Includes seven "I am" statements.

5. Several differences from synoptic Gospels: a different length of ministry for Jesus, earlier visit to Judea, different date for Passover (on the Sabbath, day after crucifixion, rather than on Friday). Twenty-four hours before crucifixion takes up one-third of book. Possibly omitted material that would be duplication, adding new material not before recorded.

Other Sources

G. Non-biblical Sources

1. Gospel According to Thomas, a manuscript discovered in 1945 along with other Gnostic and semi-Gnostic documents in Nag Hammadi in upper Egypt; other collections of Jesus' sayings dating from the second century also found in Egypt and elsewhere.

2. Jesus referred to by second century non-Christian writers. Jewish historian Josephus (in passages of doubtful authenticity) in Antiquities; Roman writers Tacitus in Annals, Seutonius in Life of Claudia, Pliny the younger in Letters, and Lucian in Death of Peregrinus.

3. Other sources:
   a. Second century Christian writings (Didache, Clement, Barnabas, Polycarp, Ignatius, Eusebius, Justin, etc.).
   b. Some references in Talmud and Koran.

III. BOYHOOD AND YOUTH OF CHRIST JESUS (Luke 1:1--2:52; Matt. 1:1--2:23)

Birth

A. Birth--7 or 6 B.C.--of Jesus (Joshua or "Yeshua", means "Saviour")

1. Birth of John the Baptist (Luke 1:5-25, 57-80).

2. Angel appearance to Mary (Luke 1:26-56)

3. Birth of Jesus (Luke 2:1-21; Matt. 1:18-25).

4. Constructions of genealogy (Matt. 1:1-17; Luke 3:23-38)

5. Consecration to God after 40 days (Luke 2:22-39).

6. Visit of the Magi (Matt. 2:1-12).

7. An unusually bright "star" appeared in 7 B.C. when Jupiter and Saturn were in close conjunction.

8. Flight to Egypt (Matt. 2:13-18; Hosea 11:1).

9. Return after Herod's death - 4 B.C. (Matt. 2:19-23).

B. Boyhood in Nazareth (Luke 2:39)

1. Lived with mother and Joseph, and younger brothers [James, Joses, Simon, Juda] and sisters (Matt. 13:55, 56; Mark 6:3).
2. Attended synagogue school in Nazareth.
3. At 12 years of age, traveled to Jerusalem to celebrate the Passover (Luke 2:40-52).

C. From Age 12 to 30 or 32 (Luke 2:51, 52).

1. Probably Jesus continued Scriptural study and led the life of a carpenter (a combination of contractor, architect, builder and cabinet maker), and became head of the family and the business at passing of Joseph.
2. Many speculations about this period. One theory has Jesus studying in India, Tibet and the British Isles (financed by Joseph of Arimathea and the gifts of the Magi)! Another theory has him a member of the Essene brotherhood. Still other theorists point out the large number of books and tracts in circulation in his time in libraries and private homes and the possibility of extensive study.
3. Jesus was a close student of the Scriptures. The Gospels record his repeating from memory sixty-one direct quotations from the Bible, making forty-three allusions to Old Testament passages, and fourteen references to events recorded in the Bible. His quotations are taken from nineteen of the thirty-nine books, the most numerous from Isaiah and Psalms.
4. Jesus was certainly literate, spoke Aramaic, read Hebrew, and possibly spoke some Greek.

IV. THE FIRST YEAR OF MINISTRY IN JUDEA (Matt. 3:1--4:11; Mark 1:1-13; Luke 3:1--4:13; John 1:1--4:42)

A. John the Baptist

1. The Baptist began preaching in Jordan valley about A.D. 26 announcing imminent coming of Messiah; John hailed as Elijah (Matt. 3:1-12; Mark 1:1-8; Luke 3:1-20; John 1:19-28).
2. Practiced baptism--ritualistic cleansing--a symbolic act signifying preparation for the new age of the Messiah.
3. Jesus came to hear John (probably A.D. 27); John recognized Jesus (his cousin) as Messiah (Matt. 3:14; John 1:29-34) but never became a follower.
4. Later doubted Jesus' Messiahship (Luke 7:19-23).
5. Jesus' praise of John the Baptist (Luke 7:24-34).
6. Career ended in prison (See Matt. 14:3-5; Mark 6:17-20; Luke 3:19, 20).

Teaching
the
Scriptures

Russell D. Robinson

New Edition
revised and expanded

Palestine

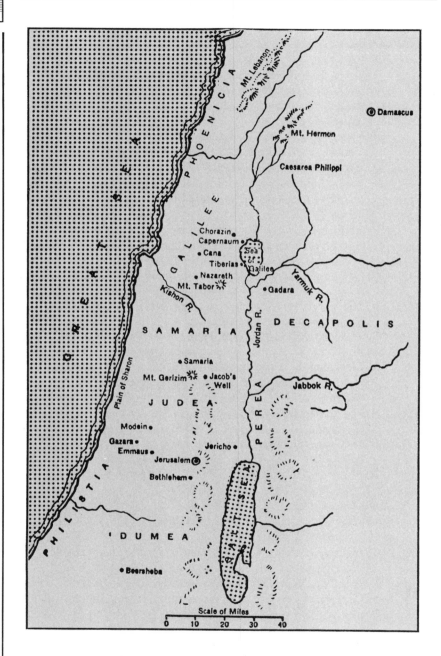

PALESTINE IN THE TIME OF JESUS

B. Baptism of Jesus (Mark 1:9-11; Matt. 3:13-17; Luke 3:21, 22; John 1:29-34)

    1. Opened a new career for Jesus who would baptize with Holy Ghost and fire (Matt. 3:11).

C. Temptation of Jesus in the Wilderness (Matt. 4:1-11; Mark 1:12, 13; Luke 4:1-13).

    1. Fasted 40 days and 40 nights.

    2. Jesus in his early thirties, probably age 32 or 33

    3. What did Messiahship mean? "If thou be the son of God...".

    4. Temptations refuted by citing Deuteronomy (8:3; 6:13; 6:16).

        a. Command stones be made bread (usher in economic abundance).

        b. Cast yourself down from the temple (impress by sign and miracle).

        c. Assume sovereignty over kingdoms of world (political kingship).

D. Beginnings of Ministry

    1. First followers: Andrew and John, then Simon (Peter), Andrew's brother, and Philip and Nathanael (John 1:35-51).

    2. Wedding at Cana (John 2:1-12).

E. Ministry in Judea (perhaps 8 months).

    1. Cleansing the Temple (John 2:13-25).

    2. Jesus and Nicodemus: the New Birth (John 3:1-21).

    3. Ministry in Judea (John 3:22--4:3).

    4. Leaves Judea on hearing of the Baptist's arrest, probably on Mount of Olives (Matt. 4:12; Mark 1:14).

F. Trip to Galilee Through Samaria

    1. Discussion with woman of Samaria at well (John 4:4-42).

V. THE SECOND YEAR OF MINISTRY IN GALILEE

(Matt. 4:12--15:20; Mark 1:14--7:23; Luke 4:14--9:17; John 4:43--6:71)

A. Beginnings of Ministry in Galilee (Matt. 4:12; Mark 1:14, 15; Luke 4:14, 15; John 4:43-45).

    1. At Cana heals nobleman's son who is sick at Capernaum (John 4:46-54).

B. Rejection at Nazareth after Address in Synagogue (Luke 4:16-30)

C. Made Headquarters in Capernaum--about 15 miles from Nazareth on the Sea of Galilee (Luke 4:31; Matt. 4:13-17)

    1. Largest commercial city of Palestine.

    2. Cosmopolitan center with active teeming population in close touch with Greco-Roman civilization.

    3. Jesus preached and healed in synagogues of Capernaum; eventually excluded by religious authorities; then preached in open spaces, fields and seashore, and the homes of friends.

Margin notes:
Baptism
Temptation
Early Ministry
Cana
Cleansed Temple
Nicodemus
"must be born again"
Samaritan Woman
Healing Boy
Rejection at Nazareth
Capernaum

Galilean Ministry	**D. Early Events**	**Matt.**	**Mark**	**Luke**
	1. The call for four "fishers of men" (Peter, Andrew, James, John)	4:18-22	1:16-20	5:1-11
	2. A Sabbath day of healing and teaching in Capernaum and healing of Peter's mother-in-law	8:14-17	1:21-34	4:31-41
First Tour of Galilee	3. **First teaching and healing tour of Galilee**	4:23-25;	1:35-39	4:42-44
	4. Healing of leprosy (man cleansed)	8:1-4	1:40-45	5:12-16
Healings	5. Healing of palsied man (paralytic let down through roof)	9:1-8	2:1-12	5:17-26
	6. Call of Matthew	9:9-13	2:13-17	5:27-32
	7. Defense of disciples for feasting rather than fasting	9:14-17	2:18-22	5:33-39

E. Return to Jerusalem for Passover (John 5:1-47)

1. Heals man at pool of Bethesda (5:1-16)

2. "My Father worketh hitherto, and I work." (5:17-24) — "I work"

3. "The hour is coming, and now is . . ." (5:25-29)

4. "I can of mine own self do nothing . . ." (5:30-47)

	F. Back in Galilee	**Matt.**	**Mark**	**Luke**
	1. Disciples plucking grain	12:1-8	2:23-28	6:1-5
	2. Healing man with withered hand	12:9-14	3:1-6	6:6-11
	3. Fame spreads	12:15-21	3:7-12	6:17-19

The Twelve

G. Choosing the Twelve

1. The first disciples had continued their occupations. Now the call to leave their nets, give up their other occupations and follow him (Matt. 4:18-22; Mark 1:16-20; Luke 5:1-11). More disciples added until there were twelve. All were Galileans except Judas Iscariot, who was a Judean.

2. The twelve (Matt 10:1-4; Mark 3:16-19; Luke 6:12-16): [1] Simon Barjona (Peter or Cephas); [2] Andrew, Peter's brother; [3] John, son of Zebedee; [4] James, John's brother; [5] Matthew (Levi); [6] Simon, the "Canaanite" (a zealot); [7] Thomas (Didymus); [8] Philip; [9] Nathanael (Bartholomew); [10] James, son of Alphaeus; [11] Thaddaeus (Lebbaeus or Judas); [12] Judas Iscariot.

Women

3. There were women disciples also including Mary Magdalene, Joanna, Susanna "and many others" (Luke 8:2,3).

4. Eventually seventy or more disciples (Luke 10:1-16).

Healing the Sick

CHRIST HEALING

H. The Sermon on the Mount--Matt. 5:1--8:1 (shorter version in Luke 6:20-49). <u>A Seven-part Sermon on the Kingdom of God</u>

1. **Attitudes open the door to the kingdom** (reign, rule of God) through desire for greater spiritual understanding and receptivity (Matt. 5:1-12).

<u>Blessed (happy) are they</u>	<u>Their reward is sure</u>
1) The poor in spirit (in need of Spirit)	Kingdom of Heaven (wisdom)
2) They that mourn (in need of healing)	Comforted (health)
3) The meek (humble)	Inherit the earth (spiritual power)
4) They that hunger and thirst after righteous- ness (seekers)	Filled (spiritual understanding)
5) The merciful (loving and kind)	Mercy (love)
6) The pure in heart (pure in thought)	See God (purity)
7) The peacemakers (peaceable)	Called children of God (holiness)

Appendix (verses 10, 11, 12) on blessing in persecution and need to rejoice (variously considered as the 8th Beatitude; the 8th and 9th; or the 8th, 9th, and 10th, the latter to correspond to the number of the Ten Commandments).

2. **Purpose in the kingdom** symbolized by "salt" which preserves quality, strength, flavor, zest and value (5:13).

3. **Activity in the kingdom**, to "let your light so shine" with good works that people may see "and glorify your Father" (5:14-16).

4. **Law in the kingdom** governs motives as well as acts, "not come to destroy, but to fulfil", re-interpreting Mosaic Laws to include motives. The standard: "Be ye therefore perfect, even as your Father which is in heaven is perfect" (5:17-48).

5. **Worship or prayers (communion) in the kingdom**--alms, prayers, and fasting done in secret, not as hypocrites (6:1-18). <u>Seven Steps of Prayer</u> (compare with tabernacle steps of Moses):

1) When thou prayest, enter into thy closet.
2) And when thou hast shut thy door . . .
3) For when ye pray, use not vain repetitions . . .for your Father knoweth what things ye have need of . . .
4) After this manner therefore pray ye: Our Father which art in heaven, Hallowed be thy name. Thy kingdom come. Thy will be done in earth, as it is in heaven.
5) Give us this day our daily bread.

Sermon on the Mount

Attitudes

Beatitudes

Purpose

Activity

Law

Worship

Lord's Prayer

6) And forgive us our debts, as we forgive our debtors.

7) And lead us not into temptation, but deliver us from evil: For thine is the kingdom, and the power, and the glory forever. [Shorter version: Luke 11:1-4]

6. **Substance in the kingdom**, spiritual treasures laid up with no anxiety or worry for the morrow; "Seek ye first the kingdom of God, and his righteousness; and all these things shall be added unto you." (6:19-34).　　Substance

7. **Justice in the kingdom** (7:1-27). It is justice:　　Justice

1) Not to judge others ("judge not"; "beam and mote").

2) Not to share holy things indiscriminately ("pearls before swine").

3) To persist in prayer ("ask . . . seek . . . knock").

4) To live by the **Golden Rule** ("Whatsoever ye would that men should do to you, do ye even so to them: for this is the law and the prophets").　　Golden Rule

5) To be steadfast and loyal ("because strait is the gate, and narrow is the way").

6) To exercise discernment ("ye shall know them by their fruits").

7) To be unshaken ("house . . . founded upon a rock").

I. The Ten Commandments as Interpreted by Jesus　　Ten Commandments

Old Testament (Moses)		New Testament (Jesus)
Deut. 6:4, 5	I-IV	Mark 12:29, 30
Ex. 20:2, 3; Deut. 5:6,7	I	Matt. 22:37, 38
Ex. 20:4-6; Deut. 5:8-10	II	John 4:24
Ex. 20:7; Deut. 5:11	III	Matt. 5:33-37
Ex. 20:8-11; Deut. 5:12-15	IV	Mark 2:27, 28
Lev. 19:18	V-X	Matt. 22:39,40
Ex. 20:12; Deut. 5:16	V	Matt. 15:3-6
Ex. 20:13; Deut. 5:17	VI	Matt. 5:21, 22
Ex. 20:14; Deut. 5:18	VII	Matt. 5:27, 28
Ex. 20:15; Deut. 5:19	VIII	Mark 10:19
Ex. 20:16; Deut. 5:20	IX	Matt. 12:35-37
Ex. 20:17; Deut. 5:21	X	Luke 12:15
New Commandment		John 13:34, 35

J. Second Tour of Teaching and Healing in Galilee　　Second Tour of Galilee Healings

	Matt.	Luke
1. Healing centurion's servant	8:5-13	7:1-10
2. Raising of widow's son at Nain		7:11-17
3. Inquiry from John the Baptist	11:2-19	7:18-35
4. Anointing of Jesus by woman in house of Simon		7:36-50
5. Jesus' companions on the tour		8:1-3

Anointing by Woman

nine

K. One Busy Day of Teaching			
and Healing	Matt.	Mark	Luke
1. Too busy to eat		3:20	
2. Accused of working by the power of the devil	12:22-37	3:21-30	(11:14-23)
3. Refuses to give a "sign" to the Pharisees	12:38-45		(11:24-36)
4. Visit of mother and brethren	12:46-50	3:31-35	8:19-21
5. Addresses parables to people:			
Parable of the sower	13:1-23	4:1-25	8:4-18
Seed growing of itself		4:26-29	
Tares and the wheat	13:24-30		
Mustard seed	13:31, 32	4:30-32	(13:18, 19)
Leaven which a woman hid	13:33		(13:20, 21)
Speaks in parables	13:34, 35	4:33, 34	
6. Parables to disciples:			
Explains tares and wheat	13:36-43		
Hidden treasure	13:44		
Pearl of great price	13:45, 46		
Net	13:47-50		
Householder	13:51, 52		
7. Stilled storm at sea	8:23-27	4:35-41	8:22-25
8. Healing of Gadarene demoniac	8:28-34	5:1-20	8:26-39

L. More Healings

	Matt.	Mark	Luke
1. Healing of woman with issue of blood and raising of Jairus' daughter	9:18-26	5:21-43	8:40-56
2. Healing of two blind	9:27-31		
3. Healing dumb man	9:32-34		
4. Harvest plenteous	9:35-38		
M. Second Rejection at Nazareth	13:54-58	6:1-6	

N. Third Tour of Galilee with Instructions to the Twelve and Sending Them Out Two by Two	10:1-- 11:1	6:7-13	9:1-6
O. Death of John the Baptist	14:1-12	6:14-29	9:7-9

P. Feeding of the Five Thousand (Matt. 14:13-23; Mark 6:30-46; Luke 9:10-17; John 6:1-15)

Q. Walking On the Water (Matt. 14:24-36; Mark 6:47-56; John 6:16-21)

R. Attempt to Proclaim Jesus King

1. Enthusiastic multitudes want to proclaim Jesus King, but he sends the crowds away and goes to a mountain to pray (John 6:14, 15; Matt. 14:22, 23).
2. Jesus says he is not a political messiah (John 6:22-27).
3. Jesus: "I am the bread of life." (John 6:28-65).
4. Many of his followers forsake him (John 6:66-69).
5. On what defiles a man; opposition of Scribes and Pharisees gains momentum (Mark 7:1-23; Matt. 15:1-20; John 7:1).

VI. THE THIRD YEAR OF MINISTRY-"JOURNEY TO JERUSALEM" (Matt. 15:21--20:34; Mark 7:24--10:52; Luke 9:18--19:28; John 7:1--11:57).

A. In Tyre and Sidon

1. Jesus is out of reach of Herod Antipas "the fox" who executed John the Baptist.
2. Healing of Syro-Phoenician woman's daughter (Mark 7:24-30; Matt. 15:21-28).

B. In Decapolis

1. Teaching, and healing of deaf mute (Mark 7:31-37; Matt. 15:29-31).
2. Feeding of 4,000 (Matt. 15:32-38; Mark 8:1-9).
3. Brief visit to Magdala (Dalmanutha) and clash with Pharisees and Sadducees (Matt. 15:39--16:4; Mark 8:10-13).
4. Healing of blind man at Bethsaida (Mark 8:22-26).
5. Warning against false leaven (Matt. 16:5-12; Mark 8:14-21).

C. At Caesarea Philippi

1. Instructions to disciples: "But whom say ye that I am?" Peter's reply (Mark 8:27-30; Matt. 16:13-20; Luke 9:18-21).
2. Foresees troubles ahead and his ultimate victory (Mark 8:31--9:1; Matt. 16:21-28; Luke 9:22-27).
3. Transfiguration (Moses and Elias [Elijah] talk with Jesus). Shows unity of Jesus' teaching with the <u>Law</u> and the <u>Prophets</u> [Scriptures] (Mark 9:2-13; Matt. 17:1-13; Luke 9:28-36).
4. After disciples fail to heal demoniac boy, Jesus heals him (Mark 9:14-29; Matt. 17:14-21; Luke 9:37-42).

D. Final Work in Capernaum

1. Foretells resurrection (Mark 9:30-32; Matt. 17:22, 23; Luke 9:43-45).
2. Pays tax with coin from fish's mouth (Matt. 17:24-27).
3. Disciples squabble as to who shall be greatest (Mark 9:33-50; Matt. 18:1-14; Luke 9:46-50).
4. Instructions on how to handle a grievance toward another; parable of the unforgiving servant (Matt. 18:15-35).
5. With trials before him, he brooks no half-way allegiance (Luke 9:57-62; Matt. 8:19-22).

Attempt to Make Jesus King

"bread of life"

Tyre and Sidon

Decapolis

"Whom Say Ye"

Transfiguration

Capernaum

Disciples Squabble

Handling Grievances

E. The Seventy (or 72)

The Seventy

    1. Instructions to the seventy (Luke 10:1-16).

    2. Results of their work and Jesus' satisfaction (Luke 10:17-20).

    3. Jesus the Son reveals the Father (Matt. 11:20-30; Luke 10:21-24).

    4. Parable of the Good Samaritan (Luke 10:25-37).

F. Visit to Jerusalem for Feast of Tabernacles.

Visit to Jerusalem

    1. Traveled through Samaria. Rejected at one town (Luke 9:51-56).

    2. Stays with Mary and Martha at Bethany (Luke 10:38-42).

    3. Secretly attends Feast. Teaches in Temple (John 7:1-52).

    4. Forgives woman adulteress (John 7:53--8:11).

"light of the world"

    5. Jesus: "I am the light of the world" (John 8:12-20).

Devil--"liar"

    6. Describes nature of sin and evil [devil "liar"] (John 8:21-59).

    7. Heals man born blind (John 9:1-41).

"good shepherd"

    8. Jesus: "I am the door of the sheep" and "I am the good shepherd" (John 10:1-21).

    9. Crosses Jordan to Perea to be out of reach of enemies.

G. Work in Perea

Perean Ministry

    1. Except for brief intervals Jesus spent four or five months in Perea "into the coasts of Judea beyond Jordan" on his "Journey to Jerusalem".

    2. Summary of early Perean Ministry.

Parables

Setting	Parable or Lesson	Luke
a. Repeats Lord's Prayer	Parable of importunate friend	11:1-13
b. Heals dumbness	Answers attack	11:14-36
c. Dining with Pharisee	Woe unto you	11:37-54
d. Crowds outside house	Nothing covered; parable of rich fool	12:1-21
e. Instructing disciples	Parables of waiting servants and wise steward	12:22-53
f. Instructing crowds	Discern signs of times	12:54-59
	Repent; parable of barren fig tree	13:1-9
g. Healing woman crippled eighteen years	Healing on the Sabbath day	13:10-17
h. Teaching in synagogues	Repeat parables of mustard seed and leaven	13:18-21
i. Tours through villages	On whether few are saved; lament over Jerusalem	13:22-35

H. Visit to Jerusalem for Feast of Dedication

Visit to Jerusalem

Oneness with Father

    1. "I and my Father are one" (John 10:22-30).

2. "Many good works have I showed you from my Father; for which of those works do ye stone me?" (John 10:31-39).
3. He escapes to Perea (John 10:40).

I. Continues Perean Ministry (John 10:41, 42).

Setting	Parable or Lesson	Luke
1. Healing man of dropsy	Parables of wedding guests and great supper	14:1-24
2. To multitudes	Count cost of discipleship	14:25-35
3. Defense before Pharisees	Parables of lost sheep, lost coin, prodigal	15:1-32
4. Teaching disciples	Parable of unjust steward	16:1-13
5. Rebuking Pharisees	Parable of rich man (Dives) and Lazarus	16:14-31
6. Talk to disciples	Parable of unprofitable servant	17:1-10
7. To Pharisees	"The Kingdom of God is within you"	17:20-21
8. To disciples	The Coming of the Christ (Parousia)	17:22-37
9. To disciples	Parables of importunate widow and Pharisee and Publican	18:1-14

Perean Ministry

J. Raising of Lazarus
1. Lazarus, brother of Mary and Martha, fell ill and passed on. Word was sent to Jesus, who came and raised him. "I am the resurrection and the life." (John 11:1-44).
2. Plot against Jesus' life (John 11:45-57). Jesus leaves area.
3. Jesus heals ten lepers (Luke 17:11-19) on journey through Samaria. One returns to give thanks. Jesus returns to Perea.

Raising of Lazarus

K. Final Ministry in Perea

Event or Lesson	Matt.	Mark	Luke
1. On marriage	19:1-12	10:1-12	
2. Blessing little children	19:13-15	10:13-16	18:15-17
3. The rich young ruler	19:16-30	10:17-31	18:18-30
4. Parable of laborers in vineyard	20:1-16		
5. Prediction of coming death	20:17-19	10:32-34	18:31-34
6. Ambitious request of James and John	20:20-28	10:35-45	

Final Perean Ministry

L. Jesus Leaves for Passover in Jerusalem
1. Travels by way of Jericho.
2. Blind Bartimaeus healed (Mark 10:46-52; Matt. 20:29-34; Luke 18:35-43).

On Way to Jerusalem

3. Zacchaeus, tax collector reformed (Luke 19:1-10).

4. Parable of faithful stewardship (Luke 19:11-28).

VII. A CAREER CONCLUDES--AND A GOSPEL BEGINS (A.D. 30)
(Matt. 21:1--28:20; Mark 11:1--16:20; Luke 19:29--24:53; John 12:1--21:25).

    A. Stayed at Bethany at Home of Mary, Martha, and Lazarus (John 12:1).

Dinner Party

    B. Dinner at Simon's House and Anointing by Mary (John 12:2-11; Matt. 26:6-13; Mark 14:3-9).

    C. Sunday

Triumphal Entry

        1. Triumphal entry into Jerusalem (Mark 11:1-11; Matt. 21:1-11; Luke 19:29-44; John 12:12-19. Also Zech. 9:9).

        2. Returned to Bethany.

    D. Monday

        1. On the way to Jerusalem cursed the barren fig tree (perhaps symbolizing barren Judaism). (Mark 11:12-14; Matt. 21:18, 19).

Cleansing
the Temple

        2. Cleansed the Temple (Matt. 21:12-17; Mark 11:15-19; Luke 19:45-48).

    E. Tuesday

        1. On the way to Jerusalem disciples surprised to see fig tree dried up (Mark 11:20-26; Matt. 21:19-22).

Teaching in
the Temple

        2. Teaching in the Temple Courts (Luke 21:37, 38).

	Matt.	Mark	Luke
a. Authority is challenged	21:23-27	11:27-33	20:1-8
b. Parable of the two sons	21:28-32		
c. Parable of wicked husbandmen	21:33-46	12:1-12	20:9-19
d. Parable of marriage of king's son	22:1-14		(14:15-24)
e. On tribute to Caesar	22:15-22	12:13-17	20:20-26
f. On resurrection	22:23-33	12:18-27	20:27-38
g. The Great Commandment	22:34-40	12:28-34	(10:25-27)
h. On the Messiah	22:41-46	12:35-37	20:39-44
i. Beware of and woe to Scribes and Pharisees	23:1-39	12:38-40	20:45-47
j. The widow's two mites		12:41-44	21:1-4

Commandments

        3. Greeks desire to see him; Jesus' last public discourse (John 12:20-50).

        4. Continued teaching at Mount of Olives in a "code" language.

5. **"The Little Apocalypse"**--the Coming of Christ to each (Parousia)--Matt. 24:1--25:46; abbreviated versions in Mark 13:1-37 and Luke 21:5-36).

   1) Be not misled by false prophets; be alert and wise and don't be fooled (Matt. 24:1-14).

   2) Be steadfast in tribulation and persecution (24:15-28).

   3) Be encouraged. In the midst of darkness and destruction, when things seem the worst, the Son of Man (Christ) appears (24:29-31).

   4) Be ready. The coming will be sudden, in an instant (24:32-41).

   5) Be watchful and keep your lamps full of oil (parable of the ten virgins) (24:42--25:13).

   6) Work. Use your talents (parable of the talents) (25:14-30).

   7) Serve. Separation of the sheep from the goats is on the basis of "Inasmuch as ye have done it unto one of the least of these my brethren, ye have done it unto me."(25:31-46).

6. Opponents plot to destroy Jesus. (Mark 14:1, 2; Matt. 26:1-5; Luke 22:1, 2).

7. Judas joins the conspirators and consents to betray his Master (Mark 14:10, 11; Matt. 26:14-16; Luke 22:3-6).

F. Wednesday

1. Day of retirement and prayer. No record is made of this day.

G. Thursday

1. Preparations for the celebration of the Passover.

2. Arrangements made to eat the Passover in an upper room at the home of Mary, the mother of John Mark (Mark 14:12-16; Matt. 26:17-19; Luke 22:7-16).

3. The meal on the eve of the Passover (**Last Supper**).

   a. Washing each disciple's feet (John 13:1-17).

   b. Points out Judas as betrayer (Mark 14:17-21; Matt. 26:20-25; Luke 22:21-23; John 13:18-30).

   c. Strife among disciples (Luke 22:24-30).

   d. Warns disciples of their desertion (Mark 14:27-31; Matt. 26:31-35; Luke 22:31-38; John 13:31-38).

   e. The bread and the cup (Mark 14:22-25; Matt. 26:26-29; Luke 22:17-20; I Cor. 11:23-26).

   f. Promises the **Comforter** (John 14:1-31).

   g. Leave upper room (John 14:31).

4. More on Comforter; concluding prayer (John 15:1--17:26).

5. Go to the Mount of Olives (Mark 14:26; Matt. 26:30; Luke 22:39; John 18:1).

6. Struggle at **Gethsemane** (Mark 14:32-42; Matt. 26:36-46; Luke 22:40-46).

Margin notes:
- "Little Apocalypse"
- Be Wise
- Be Steadfast
- Be Encouraged
- Be Ready
- Be Watchful
- Work
- Serve
- Betrayal
- Last Supper
- Comforter
- Gethsemane

Arrest	7. Judas leads soldiers to Jesus. Arrested shortly after midnight (Mark 14:43-52; Matt. 26:47-56; Luke 22:47-53; John 18:2-12). 8. Disciples scatter

H. Friday

1. Preliminary examinations by Annas the ex-high priest in the residence of Caiaphas his son-in-law in early hours (John 18:13, 14, 19-23).

Trial by Sanhedrin

2. Hurried trial and condemnation of Jesus for blasphemy by the Sanhedrin (Jewish Temple Council) with Caiaphas presiding (Mark 14:53, 55-65; Matt. 26:57, 59-68; Luke 22:54, 63, 64; John 18:24).

Peter's Denials

3. Peter's three denials during early hours (Mark 14:54, 66-72; Matt. 26:58, 69-75; Luke 22:54-62; John 18:15-18, 25-27).

4. Formal ratification of the condemnation by the Sanhedrin after dawn (Mark 15:1; Matt. 27:1; Luke 22:66-71).

5. Remorse and suicide of Judas (Matt. 27:3-10; Acts 1:18, 19).

Trial before Pilate

6. First appearance before Pilate, Roman procurator (Mark 15:2-5; Matt. 27:2, 11-14; Luke 23:1-5; John 18:28-38).

7. Sent to Herod Antipas, Tetrarch of Galilee and Perea, who was in Jerusalem (Luke 23:6-12).

8. Appears before Pilate again. Pilate submits to demand of Sanhedrin about sunrise. Condemned by Rome for treason (Mark 15:6-15; Matt. 27:15-26; Luke 23:13-25; John 18:39--19:16).

Mocking

9. Mocking of Jesus by soldiers between 6 and 9 a.m. Taken to the cross (Mark 15:16-23; Matt. 27:27-34; Luke 23:26-33; John 19:16, 17).

Crucifixion

10. **Crucifixion** 9 a.m. to 3 p.m. (Mark 15:24-37; Matt. 27:35-50; Luke 23:33-46; John 19:18-30).

11. Words on the cross.
   1) "Father, forgive them; for they know not what they do." (Luke 23:34)
   2) "Verily I say unto thee, Today shalt thou be with me in paradise." (Luke 23:43)
   3) "Woman, behold thy son!" "Behold thy mother!" (John 19:26, 27)
   4) "Eloi, Eloi, lama sabachthani?" (My God, my God, why hast thou forsaken me?) (Matt. 27:46; Mark 15:34; Psalms 22:1)
   5) "I thirst." (John 19:28)
   6) "It is finished" (John 19:30)
   7) "Father, into thy hands I commend my spirit" (Luke 23:46)

Veil Rent

12. Veil of the Temple is rent (Mark 15:38-41; Matt. 27:51-56; Luke 23:45, 47-49).

13. Preparation and burial in tomb of Joseph of Arimathaea
(Mark 15:42-47; Matt. 27:57-61; Luke 23:50-56; John
19:31-42). | Burial

14. Sabbath rest begins 6 p.m. (Matt 27:62-66; Luke 23:56).

15. Guard placed at tomb.

I. Saturday (Sabbath, and Passover). | Sabbath

    1. After the Sabbath, Mary Magdalene and others purchase
spices (after 6 p.m.) to anoint body (Mark 16:1).

J. Sunday

    1. Before sunrise, the stone is rolled away (Matt. 28:1-4).

    2. At sunrise, women visit empty tomb (Mark 16:2-8; Matt.
28:5-8; Luke 24:1-8; John 20:1).

    3. The visit of Peter and John to the tomb (John 20:2-10; Luke
24:9-12).

    4. **Resurrection** appearances. | Resurrection

        a. Jesus appears to Mary Magdalene (Mark 16:9-11; John
20:11-18). | Appears to Mary Magdalene

        b. Jesus appears to the other women (Matt. 28:9, 10).

        c. Report of the guard (Matt. 28:11-15).

        d. Appearance to the two disciples on the way to Emmaus
(afternoon) (Mark 16:12, 13; Luke 24:13-32). | Walk to Emmaus

        e. Appearance to Simon Peter (Luke 24:33-35; I Cor. 15:5).

        f. Appearance to company of disciples (except Thomas)
that night (Mark 16:14; Luke 24:36-43; John 20:19-23).

K. Later Appearances of Jesus and Instructions to Followers

    1. Appearance to disciples at Jerusalem; doubting Thomas now
convinced (John 20:24-31). | Doubting Thomas

    2. Appearance to seven disciples at Sea of Galilee; the seaside
Morning Meal and the charge to Simon Peter: "Feed my
sheep" (John 21:1-24). | Draught of Fishes and Morning Meal

    3. Instructions to Apostles and five hundred others on mountain
in Galilee (Mark 16:15-18; Matt. 28:16-20; I Cor. 15:6).

    4. Appearance to all of the Apostles (Luke 24:44-49; Acts 1:3-8;
I Cor. 15:7).

L. Ascension (Mark 16:19; Luke 24:50, 51; Acts 1:9-11) | Ascension

    1. Probably at Olivet near Bethany.

M. The Gospel is Preached (**Mark** 16:20; Luke 24:52, 53)

    1. "And they went forth, and preached every where, the Lord
working with them, and confirming the word with signs
following."

N. Summary of Jesus' Life

    1. Only about 35 days of Jesus' three year ministry are recorded
in the Gospels.

    2. "And there are also many other things which Jesus did, the
which, if they should be written every one, I suppose that even
the world itself could not contain the books that should be
written." (John 21:25)

67

nine

"Feed My Sheep"

THE DRAUGHT OF FISHES

HIS FOLLOWERS CARRY ON

(circa A.D. 30 to 47)

"And we beheld his glory, the glory as of the only begotten of the Father, full of grace and truth. . . .And of his fulness have all we received, and grace for grace."   -John 1:14, 16

I. THE EARLY CHURCH IN JERUSALEM (c. A.D. 30-35)
  A. Matthias Chosen an Apostle
    1. At a meeting of the eleven disciples and "the women", as well as Mary, the mother of Jesus, the brothers of Jesus, and others, totalling about 120 (Acts 1:12-26). | First Meeting
  B. Day of Pentecost | Pentecost
    1. Christian group receives power of Holy Ghost [Comforter, Holy Spirit like "mighty wind" and "tongues of fire"] (Acts 2:1-13).
    2. Peter's talk to the group (2:14-40).
    3. 3,000 Christians added (2:41).
    4. Description of early church (2:42-47).
  C. Peter and John | Peter and John
    1. Healing of lame man at Beautiful Gate (Acts 3:1-11).
    2. Peter's preaching (3:12-26).
    3. Peter and John arrested and released with warning (4:1-22).
    4. Their work continues; sharing of property (4:23--5:16).
    5. Again arrested and imprisoned, and escape (5:17-20).
    6. Gamaliel convinces Temple Council [Sanhedrin] to allow Peter and John to remain free, but commands them not to teach and heal (5:21-42).
  D. Stephen | Stephen
    1. One of seven chosen to be on committee to handle church business (Acts 6:1-7).
    2. Stephen preaches and heals (6:8-10). Is arrested.
    3. Tried before Temple Council [Sanhedrin] (6:11-15).
    4. Remarkable speech in self-defense before the Council (7:1-56).
    5. Stoned to death with consent of Saul [Paul] (7:57-60).
    6. Persecution of church stepped up (8:1-3).
    7. Work extended to surrounding areas (8:4).

ten

II. THE CHURCH SPREADS BEYOND JERUSALEM (c. A.D. 35-47)

   A. Philip (not the disciple)

      1. Also a member of the committee with Stephen.

      2. Preaches in Samaria (Acts 8:5-13).

      3. Peter and John join him in Samaria (8:14-25).

      4. Philip (a traveling evangelist) goes on to other areas (8:26).

      5. Shares Gospel message with Ethiopian (Acts 8:27-40).

      6. Settled in Caesarea where years later Paul stayed with him on way to Jerusalem (Acts 21:8).

   B. Peter

      1. Continues his work of healing (Acts 9:31-43) traveling to Lydda, Joppa and Caesarea.

      2. The problem when a Roman Centurian, Cornelius, desires to become a Christian (10:1-8).

      3. Peter's dream (10:9-16).

      4. Peter welcomes Cornelius and preaches to the Gentiles at Caesarea (10:17-48).

      5. Defends his actions in Jerusalem (11:1-18).

      6. Ministry to Gentiles expanded (11:19-21).

   C. Church at Antioch (Acts 11:22-30)

      1. Here followers first called "Christians".

      2. Barnabas and Saul (Paul) preached here.

      3. Regular contributions sent to mother church in Jerusalem.

   D. Persecution in Jerusalem

      1. James, the brother of John, first disciple to be martyred (Acts 12:l, 2).

      2. Peter thrown into prison and freed by prayer (12:3-18).

      3. Death of Herod Agrippa I (12:19-23).

PETER AND PAUL
(from a glass cut found in the Catacombs of Rome)

PRIMITIVE CHRISTIANITY

(circa A.D. 30 to 100)

"Upon this rock will I build my church; and the gates of hell shall not prevail against it."   -Matthew 16:18

I. THE APOSTOLIC CHURCH
A. A Resurrection Faith   The Gospel
1. Motivated by conviction that Christ was still alive, that their discipleship had not come to an end, that their fellowship and mission must be resumed.
2. They were called "Galileans", "Nazarenes", "saints", "disciples", "brethren", "believers", as those who belonged to "the Way". Later adopted name "Christian", meaning "Christ's folk".

II. AT FIRST, CHRISTIANITY A SECT OF JUDAISM
A. Jewish Christians
1. Regarded their religion as "true Judaism"--as an improvement   "true Judaism" of Judaism--"Judaism with a plus".
2. They continued daily worship and teaching in the Temple.
3. They worshipped in the Jewish synagogues, keeping the Jewish Sabbath, as well as the Christian "Lord's Day".
B. Gentile Converts to Christianity   Gentile Christians
1. Forced a decision on relationship to Judaism--over the question of whether a Gentile must first become a Jew before becoming a Christian. There were thus two groupings among the Christians: Jewish Christians and Gentile Christians, though they worshipped together.
2. Jewish Christians continued to observe the Jewish laws but the laws were not binding on Gentile Christians. By the end of the first century, Jewish Christianity had disappeared.

III. CHRISTIAN GROUPS   Christian Groups
A. Many Local Groups Gathering in Homes
1. Simplest kind of organization.
2. Variety of beliefs and practices in local groups: "ecclesia" was less an "official" church than a free "community of the Spirit"; not so much a church or religion as a way of life; a religion without creeds; a church without buildings.

3. Emphasis on works and healing and fellowship with no respect of particular persons or distinction of rank in regard to common call. Slaves and masters were equally dedicated to mutual love and service.

B. Spirit-filled People

1. Christians strove to live after the example of their Master.

IV. MEETINGS FOR WORSHIP

Sunday Service

A. On the "Lord's Day" (Sunday)--The First Day of the Week, the Day of the Resurrection

1. Service modeled after synagogue service.
   a. Singing "psalms and hymns and spiritual songs".
   b. Prayer: "The Lord's Prayer" with worshippers saying "amen".
   c. Repeating of the Shema and probably the Decalogue.
   d. Reading of the Scriptures (the Septuagint, the Greek Old Testament), by a person with the office of Reader.
   e. Interpretation. An address by some competent person was a regular feature of the service--persons who recounted the Gospel story about career and teachings of Jesus. These later written to be read in churches when speaker not present: Paul's letters, the Gospels, the Revelation, etc.--repeated use led to their being regarded as the <u>New</u> Testament as distinguished from the Old.

2. Services held early in the morning before people had to go to work, or late in the evening.

Weekday
Meetings

B. The "Love Feast" (<u>agape</u>)--the Common Meal of Fellowship

1. The common meal emphasized fellowship (<u>koinonia</u>), joy, gladness, gratitude, life-sharing.
2. Concluded with testimonies and giving of thanks (eucharist means "thanksgiving") as a memorial that recalled similar sharing by Jesus and his disciples, especially the Last Supper.
3. First held every evening, later on Wednesday and Friday eves.
4. Included offerings for the poor, widows, and orphans.

V. ADMISSION TO MEMBERSHIP

Baptism

A. Baptism

1. Immersion in water practiced as an act of repentance marking one's entrance into the Christian community.
2. Christian baptism was all that John's baptism was--repentance and moral renewal; it was also baptism by the Holy Ghost (Holy Spirit).
3. Willingness to become a new person, to acknowledge Jesus as the Messiah, was all that was required for baptism and admission to group.

B. **Voluntary Sharing of Property**
  1. Characterized early Christians.
  2. Property was held in common so those in need, and those who were giving full-time to the church, could be supported.

C. **No Specific Creed or System of Doctrine or Belief Required**

Sharing of Property

VI. RELATIONSHIP BETWEEN CHURCHES
A. **Each Group Completely Autonomous**
  1. No form of ecclesiastical organization bound the many Christian groups into a unity; their unity was through Christ.
  2. Apostles at the mother church at Jerusalem were consulted on important matters, but each group was free to direct its own affairs.

Local Autonomy

B. **Financial Contributions**
  1. Sent by outlying Gentile Christian groups to the first church in Jerusalem for the alleviation of poverty.

VII. LEADERSHIP AND ORGANIZATION
A. **Spiritual Leadership**
  1. Apostles ("one sent forth").
      a. Others along with The Twelve were called "apostles".
      b. Those particularly selected for missionary work-- preaching and healing.
      c. Early requirements for apostleship: association with Jesus and disciples and witness of the resurrection.
      d. Paul deemed himself qualified as an apostle due to his Damascus road experience.

Apostles

  2. Prophets ("one who speaks for God")
      a. Charismatic leaders, not appointed. Anyone by the spirituality of his life could become a prophet.
      b. Those possessing inner illumination and spiritual insight.
      c. Prophets were to "speak unto men to edification, and exhortation, and comfort".
      d. Prophets were healers, and looked to for counsel.

Prophets

  3. Teachers
      a. Rated by Paul next after apostles and prophets.
      b. Function was imparting instruction in "the ways of the Lord"--instruction on the career and teachings of Jesus.
      c. It is possible they also conducted a school for children after the manner of the synagogue school.

Teachers

  4. Evangelists ("gospel story teller")
      a. Traveled from group to group recounting the Gospel story of the career and teaching of Jesus.
      b. Welcomed by local groups who gathered to listen to their messages, often far into the night.
      c. Their stories became the basis for the written Gospels.

Evangelists

eleven

B. **Management and Conduct of Church Business** (Officers)

    1. <u>Elders</u> (presbyters).

        a. Men of prominence within Christian community.

        b. Conducted affairs within local organization.

        c. Selected by popular choice.

        d. Similar in function to board of elders of Jewish
           synagogue.

    2. <u>Readers</u>.

        a. Read the Scriptures at services. The earliest church had
           no priests or clergy.

    3. <u>Pastors</u> ("shepherds").

        a. Designated or appointed helpers and care givers.

    4. <u>Bishops</u> ("overseers" or superintendents)
       (and <u>Deacons</u>, "servants" or assistants).

        a. Functionaries overseeing conduct of local affairs,
           selected by the elders and subject to them.

        b. Conducted day to day church business--visited poor, and
           widows, handled benevolence.

        c. Had no spiritual authority by virtue of positions.

VIII. HEALING

A. **"Heal the Sick"**

    1. Occupied a central place in the primitive church, as in the life
       of the Master.

    2. Healing of heart and mind and soul was considered as
       important as healing of the body.

B. **"Cast out Demons"**

    1. The term demon is translated "devil" in the King James
       Version except in Acts 17:18 where it is rendered "gods".

    2. Demons believed to exist everywhere: in the air, the water,
       the earth, hovering around the house and field, on the roofs
       of houses, under the gutters, in shady spots, ruins, cemeteries,
       etc. Believed to be in the oil, bread crumbs cast on ground,
       etc.

    3. Thought to harm people who came near them, to enter the
       bodies of men and cause diseases such as blindness, epilepsy,
       fever, catalepsy, headache, nightmare, delirious fever,
       madness, leprosy, melancholy, etc.

    4. Many different types of demons or unclean spirits with
       different names according to malady caused.

C. **Early Christians Sought to Obey the Words of Jesus**

    1. "Heal the sick, cleanse the lepers, raise the dead, cast out
       demons".

THE APOSTLE PAUL
AND HIS LETTERS

(circa A.D. 34 to 66)

"Paul, called to be an apostle of Jesus Christ through the will of God . . . Unto the church of God . . . , to them that are sanctified in Christ Jesus, called to be saints, with all that in every place call upon the name of Jesus Christ our Lord . . .: Grace be unto you and peace."   -I Corinthians 1:1-3

I. PAUL'S EARLY CAREER
A. Birthplace and Lineage
    1. Born in the city of Tarsus in Cilicia at beginning of Christian era; Tarsus, about 12 miles from the Mediterranean was a city of half a million people, a busy industrial center on the river Cydnus.

Birth in Tarsus

    2. One of the three great universities located in Tarsus (others in Athens and Alexandria). Tarsus ranked first as center for the study of philosophy, its students coming from the whole empire.

    3. Parents were of the tribe of Benjamin, devout Pharisaic Jews who also had Roman citizenship (an honor exempting them from scourging and crucifixion and providing the right of appeal to the emperor's tribunal). Saul (Latin name: Paul) had at least one sister (Acts 23:16).

Parentage

B. Education of Saul (Paul)
    1. Attended synagogue school.

    2. Learned trade of tent-making (weaving tent fabric and sail cloth from goats' hair).

    3. Educated to become a rabbi. At age 15 went to Jerusalem to study under Gamaliel (a grandson and student of Hillel of the more liberal school of Judaism).

Education

    4. Paul was taught Pharisaic system of thought: the pursuit of righteousness through obedience to the Law, the Torah.

Pharisee

C. Character and Appearance
    1. Combined an unusual intellect and a splendid organizing ability with a deeply religious nature and versatile genius.

Character

    2. Jewish, Greek, and Roman elements mingled in Paul.

    3. A hard fighter, endured hardships which seem incredible; accomplished arduous journeys over burning deserts and lofty mountain passes, survived stonings and scourgings, and other perils and buffetings on land and sea (II Cor. 11:24-33).

Appearance

4. Described by early Christian writer as "a man small in size, bald-headed, bandy-legged, well-built, with eyebrows meeting, rather long nose, and with motions full of grace" (from <u>Paul and Thecla</u>).

5. His letters indicate that he considered his bodily presence weak and insignificant; also he apparently was afflicted with some sort of trouble which he called "a thorn in the flesh".

D. Conversion of Saul, c. A.D. 34

Conversion

1. Appears in Jerusalem as a persecutor of the Christians; consented to the execution of Stephen (Acts 7:58--8:3).

2. Spiritual experience (theophany) on the road to Damascus "and suddenly there shined round about him a light . . . and he trembling and astonished said, Lord, what wilt thou have me to do? And the Lord said unto him, Arise, and go into the city, and it shall be told thee what thou must do". (Acts 9:1-9; also described in Acts 22:3-16; 26:4-18).

3. His healing by Ananias (Acts 9:10-19).

4. Retired for a time to Arabia (Gal. 1:15-17).

Early Work and Opposition

5. Returned to Damascus and "preached Christ in the synagogues"; opponents seek his destruction; he escapes in basket let over wall (Acts 9:20-25; II Cor. 11:32, 33).

Instruction

6. Meets the Apostles in Jerusalem (Acts 9:26-29; Gal. 1:18, 19).

7. Continues work in Syria and Cilicia for next ten years (Gal. 1:21-24).

8. Probably about 30 years old at time of conversion. For more than 30 years he was to be the greatest spokesman for Christianity.

II. PAUL'S MISSIONARY JOURNEYS TO ASIA MINOR AND EUROPE c. A.D. 47-56

First Missionary Journey

A. Paul's First Missionary Journey c. A.D. 47-48 (Acts 12:25--14:28) about 1400 miles

1. Paul and Barnabas, accompanied by John Mark, set out from Antioch in Syria.

2. In most cities there were large Jewish communities. They visited the synagogues and talked at services.

Cyprus

3. First stop: the island of Cyprus, the city of Salamis, and then on to Paphos where the Roman proconsul, Sergius Paulus, became a Christian. Paul meets the opposition of Elymas, the sorcerer who attempted to dissuade the proconsul (Acts 13:4-12).

Perga

4. Leaving Cyprus they sail 170 miles away to Asia Minor, the city of Perga (13:13).

Antioch

5. John Mark returns to Jerusalem and Paul and Barnabas travel north to another Antioch in Pisidia to preach in the synagogue (13:14-44).

the apostle Paul and his letters

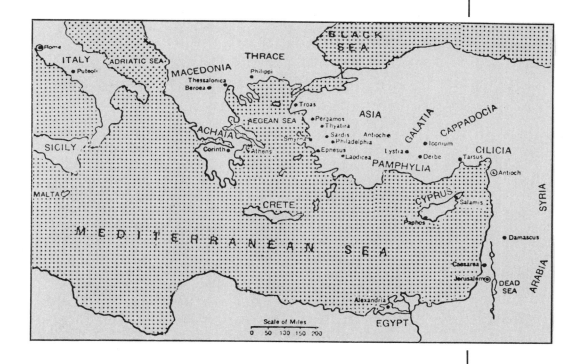

THE WORLD OF PAUL

Iconium

6. Driven out of Antioch they go sixty miles east to Iconium (Acts 13:45--14:5).

Lystra

7. Forced out of Iconium they go to Lystra and Derbe. Paul heals crippled man in Lystra (14:6-18).

8. Opponents from Antioch and Iconium come to Lystra and rouse people against Paul and Barnabas, stone Paul and leave him for dead (14:19-20).

Derbe

9. Paul recovers and they go to Derbe. Revisits cities to talk to converts (14:21-25).

10. Paul and Barnabas return to Antioch in Syria, their home church (14:26-28).

Council at Jerusalem

B. Council at Jerusalem c. A.D. 48 (Gal. 2:1-10; Acts 15:1-35)

1. Question: Must Gentiles become Jews before they can become Christians?

2. Test Case: Paul's young disciple Titus, an uncircumcised Greek.

3. Paul and Barnabas of Antioch argue the case before the church leaders in Jerusalem--James (Jesus' brother who is now head of the Jerusalem church), Peter and John.

4. Jewish Christians demand circumcision of Titus; Paul and Barnabas oppose the circumcision of Gentiles; Apostles take the middle position for sake of harmony, and compromise.

Decision

5. Decision: Divide the Field. Paul and Barnabas will preach to the Gentiles free of circumcision. Apostles will work among the Jews. Paul to remember the poor brethren in Jerusalem with contributions.

New Crisis

6. New Crisis in Antioch (Gal. 2:11-21) over fellowship between Jewish Christians and the Gentile Christians, particularly eating together. Question brought to a head by Peter's visit to Antioch. Peter, Barnabas and others withdraw from liberal position. But church again brought to Paul's view. Perhaps the four restrictions on Gentile converts in Acts 15:23-29 were the outcome of this encounter.

Second Missionary Journey

C. Paul's Second Missionary Journey c. A.D. 49-52 (Acts 15:36--18:22) about 3500 miles

1. Paul and Barnabas separate. Barnabas and John Mark go to Cyprus. Paul and Silas go overland by way of Tarsus visiting churches along the way (Acts 15:36-41).

Lystra

2. At Lystra, the 15 year-old Timothy joins Paul and Silas as they visit Christian groups (16:1-10).

Troas

3. At Troas, Luke (the writer of Acts) joins the party. [Note his use of "we" (Acts 16:11).]

Philippi

4. They go by ship to Macedonia (Greece) in Europe. At Philippi a church is formed with help of Lydia, a Gentile convert (16:12-15).

5. Paul heals girl of soothsaying and Paul and Silas are beaten and thrown into prison. They sing and are freed and return to house of Lydia (Acts 16:16-40).

6. From Philippi they go to Thessalonica 100 miles west and preach in the synagogue (17:1-13).

7. They go to Berea where Silas and Timothy remain while Paul goes by ship on to Athens (17:14, 15).

8. On Mars Hill, Paul addresses the Athenians (17:16-34).

9. Then he goes to Corinth, fifty miles west of Athens and spends a year and a half with Aquila and Priscilla (18:1-18).

10. On his return to his home church at Antioch, he travels by ship to Jerusalem to give a report to the Apostles (18:19-22).

D. Letters to the Thessalonians (about A.D. 50)

   1. <u>First Letter to the Thessalonians</u>. (Written from Corinth to the group at Thessalonica, the capitol of Macedonia, which he and Silas and Timothy had established. The letter is in response to a report brought back to Paul by Timothy whom Paul had sent to visit the group. This letter is the earliest surviving Christian literature.)

      a. Gratitude for their love and good works (I Thess. 1:1-10).

      b. Recalls his ministry with them with gratitude (2:1-16).

      c. Desires to visit them (2:17-20).

      d. Tells of report of Timothy (3:1-13).

      e. Living to please God, not sensuality (4:1-12).

      f. Christ's Coming (<u>Parousia</u>)--the Day of the Lord (4:13--5:11).

      g. Advice to the church members (5:12-22).

      h. Benedictions (5:23-28).

   2. <u>Second Letter to the Thessalonians</u>. (Written from Corinth or Athens a few months after the first letter.)

      a. Thanksgiving and prayer (II Thess. 1:1-12).

      b. Christ's Coming (<u>Parousia</u>)--the Day of the Lord (2:1-12).

      c. Be steadfast and patient in well-doing (2:13--3:5).

      d. Warns idlers to follow his example and work (3:6-16).

      e. Paul's personal signature (3:17-18).

E. Letter to the Galatians (about A.D. 52)

   1. Written from Antioch, after Paul's return from his second journey, to the four churches in Galatia (the Antioch in Pisidia, Iconium, Lystra, and Derbe). Paul founded the churches and had visited them twice since. Members were mostly converted Gentiles. Jewish Christians had visited the churches, denied the validity of Paul's teachings and required the Gentiles to obey the Mosaic laws. The letter is a "Declaration of Independence" from Judaism.

Margin notes:
- Freed from Prison
- Thessalonica
- Berea
- Athens
- Corinth
- Jerusalem
- I Thessalonians
- Earliest Surviving Christian Literature
- II Thessalonians
- Galatians
- "Declaration of Independence"

Galatians

2. Message: The Law and Christianity.
  a. Salutation (Gal. 1:1-5).
  b. Justification of his knowledge by revelation (1:6-24).
  c. Account of settling the question of whether Gentiles must become Jews to be Christians (2:1-14).
  d. Salvation "by the faith of Jesus Christ", not by observance of Jewish Law (2:15--3:5).
  e. Christians are the true heirs of Abraham (3:6-18).
  f. Law served as temporary tutor "our schoolmaster to bring us unto Christ" (3:19-29).
  g. We are now sons and heirs in Spirit (4:1-7).
  h. We cannot turn back to legalism (4:8-31).
  i. Call to freedom, guided by the Spirit, "if we live in the Spirit, let us also walk in the Spirit" (5:1--6:10).
  j. Personal autograph (6:11-18).

Third Missionary
Journey

F. **Paul's Third Missionary Journey, c. A.D. 52-56** (Acts 18:23--21:17) about 4000 miles
  1. Visits churches on the way to Ephesus (Acts 18:23).
  2. Apollos is converted by Aquila and Priscilla (18:24-28).
  3. Paul's three-year stay at Ephesus (c. A.D. 53-56).

Ephesus

  a. For three months preached in the synagogue (19:1-8).
  b. Forced out of the synagogue, he hired his own lecture hall, the Hall of Tyrannus, and taught in the afternoons and possibly evenings for two years. In the morning he practiced his trade of tent-making (Acts 19:9, 10; I Cor. 4:11-16).
  c. Paul becomes widely known for his healing work (Acts 19:11-20).
  d. Paul plans to go to Macedonia and sends Timothy and Erastus on ahead (Acts 19:21, 22; I Cor. 4:17-19).
  e. Opposition of silversmiths (who made images of Greek goddess) grows. They organize a riot which the town clerk brings to an end (Acts 19:23-41).

Corinth

  4. Paul leaves Ephesus and goes to Corinth, staying there three months, then returns to Troas where he and Luke meet Timothy and other workers who had gone on ahead (Acts 20:1-6).

Troas

  5. While preaching at Troas, Paul restores Eutychus who accidently fell from the third story (20:7-12).
  6. Leaving Troas, Paul walks 19 miles to a seaport where he is picked up by a ship that the others were on [possibly a plan to elude enemies] (Acts 20:13-16).

Miletus

  7. At Miletus Paul holds a meeting of the leaders of the churches in Ephesus and gives farewell address (20:17-38).

Jerusalem

  8. Despite warnings of danger, Paul then goes to Jerusalem (21:1-17).

G. The Corinthian Correspondence

1. First Letter (II Cor. 6:14--7:1). (Written from Ephesus about A.D. 53 to the church at Corinth, founded by Paul and Silas, Timothy, Aquila and Priscilla. Group included Jewish Christians and Greek Christians [Gentile Christians]. Only a fragment of the letter remains.) — II Corinthians

   a. Avoid entanglement with unbelievers, bad company that might lead a true Christian astray (II Cor. 6:14--7:1).

2. Second Letter (all of I Corinthians). (Written from Ephesus about A.D. 54). — I Corinthians

   a. Salutation (I Cor. 1:1-9).

   b. Avoid factions and divisions in church (1:10--4:21). — Factions

   c. Avoid immorality and general bad conduct (5:1--6:20).

   d. On marriage, divorce, and celibacy (7:1-40). — Marriage

   e. On eating meat from pagan sacrifices (8:1--9:27).

   f. Avoid all ties to idolatry (10:1--11:1).

   g. Tradition that women cover head in church (11:2-16).

   h. On abuses of the Love Feast (agape) and the Lord's Supper (11:17-34).

   i. The gifts of the Spirit "diversities of gifts but the same Spirit"; all members of the body of the Church of Christ "many members, yet one body" (12:1-31). — "gifts of Spirit"

   j. Love, the greatest gift: "faith, hope, charity [love], these three; but the greatest of these is charity". (13:1-13). — Greatest: love

   k. Speak understandably when testifying in church, "speak unto men to edification, and exhortation, and comfort". (14:1-40). — Speaking in Church

   l. The resurrection--"put on immortality" (15:1-58).

   m. Travel plans and Christian greetings (16:1-24).

3. Third Letter (II Cor. 10:1--13:14). (Written from Ephesus about A.D. 55 after a visit to Corinth where he was spurned.) — II Corinthians

   a. Defense of his ministry (II Cor. 10:1--12:21). — Defense

   b. Ultimatum to Corinthian church: "examine yourselves", "do no evil", "be perfect", "be on one mind" (13:1-14).

4. Fourth Letter (II Cor. 1:1--6:13; 7:2--9:15). (Written from Macedonia about A.D. 55 upon hearing from Titus of the Corinthians' repentance and reformation. A letter of warm affection.)

   a. Gratitude to God for their reformation (II Cor. 1:1-11).

   b. Changes in travel plans (1:12--2:13).

   c. Explains his ministry (2:14--4:6).

   d. Look "at the things which are not seen" (4:7--5:10).

   e. Be an "ambassador for Christ", a "new creature" in Christ for "now is the day of salvation" (5:11--6:13). — Ambassador for Christ

   f. Paul's confidence and joy in them (7:2-16).

   g. Request for funds for Jerusalem church (8:1--9:15).

81

H. Letter to the Romans

1. Written from Corinth about A.D. 56. Paul had not yet been to Rome, but had heard of the group there.
2. A treatise in letter form to unite Greek and Jew. Sometimes called "The Gospel According to Paul".
   a. The saving righteousness of God (Rom. 1:1-17).
   b. All men need righteousness (salvation) (1:18--3:20).
   c. Man freed from sin by faith, not the Law (3:21--5:11).
   d. Death through Adam and life through Christ, "yield yourselves unto God" (5:12--6:23).
   e. Freedom from the Law in new life in Christ (7:1-25).
   f. New life assures victory over the carnal mind, "the law of the Spirit of life in Christ Jesus hath made me free from the law of sin and death" (8:1-39).
   g. God's promise to Israel: righteousness for all (9:1--11:36).
   h. Righteousness in daily life when "transformed by the renewing of your mind" (12:1--15:13).
   i. Paul's plans for further work (15:14-33).
   j. Greetings to Christians (16:1-27). (Some scholars believe this not a part of the letter to the Romans, but rather a letter of recommendation for Phoebe written to the church at Ephesus.)

III. PAUL'S ARREST AND WORK AS A PRISONER c. A.D. 56-61

A. Paul in Jerusalem c. 56

1. Opposition to Paul came from both within and without the Church--from Christian Jews as well as non-Christian Jews for he renounced the Law.
2. Paul reports to the Apostles on his Gentile mission (Acts 21:17-19).
3. To appease Jewish Christians Paul consents to perform the Hebrew Temple Vow of the Nazarite (21:20-26).
4. As a result Paul's enemies claim he polluted the Temple (21:27-29).
5. A riot results and Paul is about to be beaten to death (21:30-32).
6. Paul is rescued by Roman soldiers who arrest him (21:33-36).
7. Paul receives permission to speak to the mob (21:37--22:24).
8. About to be scourged he demands his rights of Roman citizenship (22:25-30).
9. Appears before the Jewish Council (the Sanhedrin) and again is rescued by Roman soldiers (23:1-10).
10. Paul knows God is with him (23:11).
11. Warned by his sister's son of a plot against him, Paul is taken in custody to Caesarea by night (23:12-33).

B. Paul in Caesarea c. 56-58

    1. Trial before Felix, the Roman Governor. Because of Jewish opposition Felix fears to release him, so keeps Paul a prisoner. (Acts 23:34--24:27).

    2. Later Festus becomes governor. Trial before Festus and Paul's appeal to Caesar for justice (25:1-12).

    3. At the request of Festus, Paul appears before the Herodian King Agrippa. (25:13--26:32).

C. Journey to Rome c. 58-59 about 2,000 miles

    1. Paul, along with other prisoners, starts for Rome under Roman guard Julius. Luke and Aristarchus accompany him. (Acts 27:1-5).

    2. After stormy voyage, they transfer to another ship and reach island of Crete (27:6-13).

    3. Upon leaving Crete, they meet the full force of the storm. (27:14-40).

    4. After 14 days of being blown off course 500 miles, the ship is wrecked on the island of Melita (Malta) but everyone of the crew was saved as Paul assured them (27:41--28:1).

    5. During stay at Malta, Paul heals himself of serpent bite, and heals many sicknesses of the people (28:2-10).

    6. Three months later they set out on another ship for Italy, making some stops along the way (28:11-13).

    7. Embarks at Puteoli where Paul is met by Christian friends. He is welcomed by Christians as he travels the Appian Way to Rome (28:14-16).

D. Paul in Rome c. 59-61

    1. Awaiting trial before Nero, Paul lives in rented house, guarded by a soldier. He receives friends and preaches the gospel freely to all who come to him (Acts 28:17-31) and carries on correspondence with the churches he founded.

E. Paul's Correspondence from Rome c. 59-61

    1. Letter to the Colossians. (Written to the church at Colossae, about 100 miles inland from Ephesus. Paul had never been to Colossae. The founder of the group, Epaphras, visited Rome, asking Paul's advice, apparently was imprisoned, and Paul sent the letter back by the hand of Tychicus. A refutation of false teachings, arbitrary observances and extreme asceticism in worship, and of various attempts to add new elements to Christian faith and worship.)

        a. Salutation and prayer (Col. 1:1-14).

        b. Urges strict adherence to simple faith of Christ Jesus (1:15--2:3).

        c. No need for extraneous theory or ritualism (2:4-23).

        d. The real need: Christian living (3:1--4:6).

        e. Greetings and farewell (4:7-18).

Margin notes:
In Caesarea
Trials

Journey to Rome

Shipwreck

Paul in Rome
House Arrest

Colossians

Christian Living

Philemon

Onesimus
Runaway Slave

Ephesians

All Men One

Put on New Man

Armor of God

Philippians

Unity and Humility

2. <u>Letter to Philemon</u>. (Written to Philemon, a rich leading member of the Church of Colossae, about Philemon's slave Onesimus who had run away from him and come under Paul's influence in Rome. A personal letter.)

   a. Paul asks Philemon to receive his slave as a Christian brother, and Paul promises to make good anything Onesimus may have stolen.

3. <u>Letter to the Ephesians</u>. (Most scholars agree this letter was written by Paul, probably as a circular letter to reach various churches in Asia, as well as Ephesus. Also possibly it is the letter to the church of Laodicea mentioned in Col. 4:16. Some believe it was written later by a disciple of Paul, as an introduction to a collection of Pauline letters.)

   a. Salutation (Eph. 1:1-2).

   b. Men are predestined for blessing and redemption (1:3-14).

   c. A prayer for spiritual understanding (1:15-23).

   d. In Christ, God has made all men one (2:1--3:13).

   e. A prayer "to be strengthened with might by his Spirit in the inner man; that Christ may dwell in your hearts . . . that ye might be filled with all the fulness of God". (3:14-21).

   f. "Walk worthy of the Lord" in unity (4:1-16).

   g. Put off the "old man" and "put on the new"; "walk as children of light" (4:17--5:21).

   h. The Christian household (5:22--6:9).

   i. "Put on the whole armor of God" (6:10-20).

   j. Personal note and benediction (6:21-24).

4. <u>Letter to the Philippians</u>. (Written to church at Philippi in Macedonia founded by Paul on his first visit to Europe where Lydia had become one of the first Christians. Written in response to a generous sum contributed by the group and sent to Paul via Epaphroditus. Epaphroditus became ill and after being healed by Paul returned to Philippi with this letter.)

   a. Greetings and a prayer (Phil. 1:1-11).

   b. Outcome of trial will soon be known; determined to meet it with joy (1:12-30).

   c. Maintain unity through Christlike humility and "let this mind be in you, which was also in Christ Jesus" (2:1-18).

   d. Personal note on Timothy and Epaphroditus (2:19-30).

   e. Warning against Judaizers; yield the whole life to Christ and press toward the goal (3:1-21).

   f. Be steadfast, thankful, joyful, think on good things (4:1-9).

   g. Thanks for gifts sent him (4:10-23).

IV. PAUL'S LATER YEARS AND THE LETTERS TO TITUS AND TIMOTHY, c. 61-66

    A. Two Traditions About Paul's Later Years Paul's Later Years

        1. That Paul's trial resulted in conviction and he was martyred about A.D. 61 (in which case the letters to Titus and Timothy were written by someone else).

        2. That Paul's trial resulted in acquittal before Nero as Paul had hoped (Phil. 1:26; 2:24), and that he continued his missionary activity and writings (see Titus 3:12-14; II Tim. 1:15). It is possible, though unlikely, that he went to Spain as he once planned (Rom. 15:28). Paul was later martyred, probably sometime around A.D. 66.

Martyrdom

    B. The First Letter to Timothy I Timothy

        1. Paul writing from Macedonia to Timothy (son of a Greek father and a Jewish mother), who became Paul's special protege and loyal assistant, accompanying Paul on various missions; now at Ephesus.

            a. Importance of sound teaching (I Tim. 1:1-20). Church Affairs

            b. Public worship of the church (2:1-15).

            c. Qualifications of church superintendents and assistants (translated "bishops" and "deacons") (3:1-13).

            d. Condemnation of asceticism (3:14--4:5).

            e. Teach Christian conduct and "be a good minister of Jesus Christ" and "let no man despise thy youth" (he was about 30 years old) (4:6--6:21).

    C. Letter to Titus Titus

        1. Written to Titus, a Greek convert (some believe he was the brother of Luke); apparently helped Paul found a church in Crete, where he receives this letter.

            a. Qualifications of elders and superintendents ("bishops") (Titus 1:1-16).

            b. On teaching Christian conduct to the congregation (2:1--3:11).

            c. Personal (3:12-15).

    D. Second Letter to Timothy (Paul's last letter) II Timothy

        1. Written from Rome where Paul is awaiting the sentence of death, to his loved Timothy still at Ephesus.

            a. Salutation (II Tim. 1:1-2). Last Letter

            b. "Stir up the gift of God, which is in thee" (1:3-18).

            c. "Endure hardness, as a good soldier in Jesus Christ" (2:1-13).

            d. "Study to shew thyself approved unto God . . . and shun profane and vain babblings . . . follow righteousness, faith, charity, peace" (2:14--3:9).

            e. Paul's charge to Timothy (3:10--4:5).

            f. "I have finished my course" (4:6-22).

twelve

Apostle
to the Gentiles

PAUL

THE LETTER TO THE HEBREWS

"God, who at sundry times and in divers manners spake in time past unto the fathers by the prophets, Hath in these last days spoken unto us by his Son."
-Hebrews 1:1, 2

I. THE LETTER TO JEWISH CHRISTIANS

A. Authorship

1. Almost universally, scholars agree that this letter was not written by Paul, though it is certainly Pauline in character.
2. Perhaps written by an associate of Paul. Various fascinating speculations attribute the letter to such figures as Barnabas, Luke, Silas, Apollos, or Priscilla, but there is no way of knowing.
3. The letter was probably written about A.D. 67 before the fall of Jerusalem (or perhaps later) to Christian Jews living in a large city (perhaps Rome).

B. Message

1. Christ Jesus has fulfilled Jewish ideas; no need to relapse into Judaism. Christ Jesus brought the new covenant, the new agreement, which surpasses the old agreement of the Law.
2. Sonship of Christ Jesus, God's final revelation (Heb. 1:1--2:8).
3. Sonship of Christ Jesus superior to Law of Moses as means of salvation (2:9--3:6).
4. Danger of unbelief and inaction (3:7--4:13).
5. Christ Jesus is the "called of God, a high priest after the order of Melchisedek" and supersedes the Levitical priesthood (4:14--7:28).
6. The Son ministers in the heavenly sanctuary which supersedes the old tabernacle [Temple] (8:1--10:18).
7. Let us enter this sanctuary (10:19-39).
8. The achievements of men of faith--"the substance of things hoped for, the evidence of things not seen" (11:1-40).
9. "Let us run with patience the race that is set before us, looking unto Jesus the author and finisher of our faith" (12:1-17).
10. You are come "unto the city of the living God, the heavenly Jerusalem" (12:18-29).
11. Serve and worship within the fellowship, "make you perfect in every good work to do his will" (13:1-25).

Authorship

Hebrews

New Covenant

Final Revelation

New High Priest

New Sanctuary

Men of Faith

New Jerusalem

thirteen

"God is love"

THE APOSTLE JOHN

LETTERS OF JAMES, PETER, JUDE AND JOHN

"Beloved, now are we the sons of God, and it doth not yet appear what we shall be: but we know that, when he shall appear, we shall be like him; for we shall see him as he is."   -I John 3:2

I. THE LETTER OF JAMES
A. Authorship
1. Quite probably by James, the brother of Jesus, who was head of the Church in Jerusalem for about twenty years. Possibly written about A.D. 50-60 to the true spiritual Israel "the twelve tribes which are scattered abroad." (Some scholars believe the book was written much later by someone other than James.)

B. Message Closely Echoes the Teaching of Jesus
1. The test of faith (James 1:1-18).
2. Hearing and practicing God's word (1:19--2:13).
3. Relationship between faith and action (2:14-26).
4. Controlling the tongue (3:1-18).
5. Worldliness a liability (4:1--5:6).
6. Patience and prayer (5:7-20).

II. THE FIRST LETTER OF PETER
A. Authorship
1. Peter, one of the original Twelve, writing through Sylvanus (Silas) probably from Rome described as "Babylon". Addressed to Jewish Christians in various parts of Asia Minor. Written almost certainly in A.D. 64., shortly before martyrdom.

B. Peter's Letter a Message of Hope ("hope" was to Peter what "faith" was to Paul, "works" to James, and "love" to John)
1. Following Christ will bring rewards (I Peter 1:1-13).
2. "As newborn babes, desire the sincere milk of the word that you may grow thereby" (1:14--2:8).
3. You are "a chosen generation, a royal priesthood, an holy nation, a peculiar people" (2:9-17).
4. Advice to slaves (2:18-25).
5. Advice to married Christians (3:1-7).
6. Be faithful under persecution (3:8--4:19).
7. Continue in love; your reward is sure (5:1-14).

Margin notes:
Authorship

James

Faith

Works
Tongue

I Peter

"a lively hope"

fourteen

III. THE SECOND LETTER OF PETER
    A. Authorship
        1. Most scholars believe this letter was not written by Peter, the Apostle. It is usually dated late, around A.D. 130.

II Peter

    B. Message
        1. True knowledge is found only in Christ Jesus (II Peter 1:1-21).
        2. Beware of false prophets (2:1-22).
        3. "The promise of his coming" (3:1-18).

IV. THE LETTER OF JUDE
    A. Authorship
        1. Possibly written by Jude, the brother of Jesus, between A.D. 70 and 80. However, many scholars place it as late as the second century, along with II Peter.

Jude

    B. Message
        1. Counteracts false teachings of a group that felt that because all matter was evil and not of God, therefore one's actions did not affect one's spiritual life, thus one could excuse evil living.
        2. Jude refers to the apocalyptic Book of Enoch (1:14) and the Assumption of Moses (1:9), two early books in wide use, rejected by the rabbis and not given canonical status.

V. THE LETTERS OF JOHN
    A. Authorship

John

        1. Written by the author of the Gospel of John, probably John the Disciple. (Some authorities attribute the letters and Gospel to John, the Elder, an associate of the Disciple.) Tradition that the Disciple lived to a very old age, in last years in Ephesus authored the Gospel, the three letters and the book of Revelation. Tradition also that John experienced a miraculous deliverance from a caldron of boiling oil to which he had been condemned during a persecution.
        2. Letters dated A.D. 80 to 90.

I John

    B. Message of First Letter of John
        1. Prologue: The Word of Life (I John 1:1-4).
        2. God is light and in Him no darkness (1:5-10).
        3. Live in the light of Truth and be on guard against sin (2:1-29).
        4. Now are we the children of God (3:1-3).
        5. Victory of the Children of God (3:4--4:6)

"God is Love"

        6. God is Love, to love God is to love one another (3:4--4:21).
        7. Epilogue: The true God and eternal Life (5:1-21).
    C. Messages of Other Two Letters of John (personal letters to individuals)

II John
III John

        1. Live in Truth and Love (II John).
        2. Follow the Truth (III John).

THE APOCALYPSE OF JOHN

"And I saw a new heaven and a new earth . . . And I John saw the holy city, new Jerusalem, coming down from God out of heaven."   -Revelation 21:1, 2

I. BACKGROUND OF THE BOOK

A. Authorship

1. Tradition ascribes the book to the disciple John, the author of the Gospel and the three letters. (Some scholars dispute this, ascribing the books attributed to the Disciple to one or more others named John.)
2. Probably written around A.D. 90 after the Fall of Jerusalem, during the persecutions of the Christians by Domitian; possibly earlier (some scholars date it later).
3. Written while author was exiled in the island of Patmos, off the coast from Ephesus.

B. Apocalyptic Writing

1. A style of literature written in code used by the Hebrews. Written to give courage and inspiration of the ultimate triumph of good in the midst of persecution.
2. Examples of apocalyptic writing in Old Testament in parts of Isaiah, Daniel, Ezekiel, Jeremiah, Zechariah, Joel and Malachi.
3. Written in figurative language--symbols--imagery--a code-language or picture language. A metaphor or allegory--vision literature not meant to be taken literally, that in fact becomes nonsense when taken literally.
4. The reader (who knew the meaning of the symbols--who could decode it) translated the symbols into a powerful message of assurance and hope--the certain triumph of good over evil.

C. The Message of John

1. John called his apocalypse "The Revelation of Jesus Christ which God gave unto him, to shew unto his servants things which must shortly come to pass; and he sent and signified it by his angel unto his servant John who bare record of the word of God, and of the testimony of Jesus Christ, and of all things that he saw" (Rev. 1:1,2).
2. His book is carefully constructed, on an almost mathematical plan. The key is the number seven, the Hebrew symbol of completeness.

Authorship

Apocalyptic Writing

Message of John

Seven-fold
Structure

3. The literary design uses the Hebrew literary device of the seven-fold structure:

The fourth is the climax, or most important point, with the first three preparing the way for the fourth, and the last three a natural result of the fourth.

4. John draws heavily from the Old Testament for his code language--symbols his readers would understand. Of the 404 verses of the Apocalypse, 278 of them contain reference to the Old Testament.

5. His word-picture symbols may be categorized as either types of Truth or types of falsity, types of good or types of evil.

Scenes in Thought

6. The scenes of the Revelation take place in thought--in human consciousness. They illustrate the warfare in thought by which Truth overcomes deception, in which the full knowledge of God destroys all ignorance concerning Him.

7. The purpose of the book was not to look down the centuries (with some secret scheme of the ages hidden in the text); rather it was to assure the suffering saints that relief was at hand (Rev. 1:3).

D. A Fitting Climax to Holy Scripture

Climax of
Scripture

1. Reaffirms the glory of God's creation with which the Bible opens and triumphantly reverses the account of man's fall, for "that old serpent, called the Devil, and Satan, which deceiveth the whole world" has been utterly destroyed by Christ. (Compare with Gen. 2:4--4:26).

2. Contrast the unfoldment of the seven visions with the Revelation of Creation in Gen. 1:1--2:3.

1) <u>One on the Throne, the Lamb, and the Seven-Sealed Book</u>
"Let there be light"

2) <u>The Lamb Opens the Seven Seals</u>
"Let there be a firmament . . . and let it divide the waters"

3) <u>Seven Trumpets Announce the Coming End of Evil</u>
"Let the dry land appear . . . and let the earth bring forth fruit"

4) <u>The Woman, the Man-Child, and Persecution by the Dragon</u>
"Let there be lights in the firmament"

5) <u>Seven Vials of Judgment Poured out and the Destruction of Babylon</u>
"Let the waters bring forth abundantly . . . and

fowl that fly above the earth"
6) <u>Triumph of the Word of God, Destruction of the Dragon, and the End of Evil</u>
"Let the earth bring forth the living creature . . . Let us make man in our image . . . and let them have dominion"
7) <u>The New Jerusalem--The Holy City Appears</u>
"Thus the heavens and the earth were finished"

II. THE BOOK: "REVELATION OF JESUS CHRIST"
A. Preface to the Revelation
1. Title page of book (Rev. 1:1-3).
2. Introductory prayer (1:4-8).
3. Appearance of the Risen Christ to John and instructions to write (1:9-20).
B. Prologue: The Seven-fold Message to the Church--The Risen Christ speaks to the Churches (to thought)

Church	Evil to be Overcome	Reward for Overcoming
1. Ephesus	Unfaithfulness	Tree of life
2. Smyrna	False teachings	No Harm from second death
3. Pergamos	Immorality	Hidden manna, white stone, new name
4. Thyatira	Willful domination	Morning star
5. Sardis	Unwatchfulness	White raiment, name in book of life
6. Philadelphia	Lack of love	Pillar in God's temple, new name
7. Laodicea	Lukewarmness	The right to reign with God

C. The Seven Visions
1. **The First Vision: One on the Throne, the Lamb, and the Seven-Sealed Book** (Rev. 4:1--5:10).
Scene: A door opened in heaven (4:1).
1) One on the throne is supreme (4:2, 3).
2) Twenty-four elders (interpreters) in white raiment on surrounding seats (4:4).
3) Seven lamps of fire, the seven Spirits of God (4:5).
4) Sea of glass before the throne, and four beasts (living creatures) in the midst and around the throne (4:6-8).
5) Song of worship of the One on the throne: All things created by and for God (4:9-11).
6) Seven sealed book (scroll) sealed with seven seals in the right hand of One on throne (5:1-5).

Preface

Prologue: Rewards of Overcoming

Acknowledgment of God, Christ, and the Scriptures

93

Teaching
the
Scriptures

Russell D. Robinson

The Christ
Uncovers the
Sins that Seal
the Scriptures

7) Lamb appears and takes the book from the One on the throne and is found worthy to open the seven-sealed book (5:6-10).

2. **The Second Vision: The Lamb Opens the Seven Seals** (Rev. 5:11--8:1)

Scene: Angels in heaven sing of the Lamb's worthiness to open the seals (5:11-14).

1) First seal: white horse and rider with bow and crown; determination to conquer (lust) (6:1, 2).
2) Second seal: red horse and rider with great sword; war and destruction (revenge) (6:3, 4).
3) Third seal: black horse and rider with balances; famine; starvation wages (covetousness) (6:5, 6).
4) Fourth seal: pale horse whose rider's name is death; hell follows with him (envy) (6:7, 8).
5) Fifth seal: martyrs calling for rewards; a subtle sin (self-righteousness) (6:9-11).
6) Sixth seal: earthquakes and darkness and destruction on earth (self-will); and Children of Israel, Servants of God, sealed (protected), except Dan (6:12--7:17).
7) Seventh seal: silence in heaven (self-ignorance) (8:1).

Destruction of
Evil Begins With
Resurrection of
Thought

3. **The Third Vision: Seven Trumpets Announce the Coming End of Evil** (Rev. 8:2--11:19)

Scene: Angels in heaven prepare to blow the trumpets to announce the coming end of evil on earth (8:2-6).

1) First trumpet: hail and fire upsets earth (8:7).
2) Second trumpet: burning mountain falls into sea (8:8, 9).
3) Third trumpet: burning star turns river to wormwood (8:10, 11).
4) Fourth trumpet: sun, moon, and stars darkened (8:12, 13).
5) Fifth trumpet: bottomless pit opened from which locusts emerge to torment men (first woe) (9:1-12).
6) Sixth trumpet: four angels of the Euphrates loosed and a great army of invaders kill a third of men; and a "mighty angel" appears with a "little book open" and a "reed like unto a rod"; power is given unto the "two witnesses", though persecuted and killed, they are resurrected and ascend to heaven; then a great earthquake occurs and a tenth part of the city falls (second woe) (9:13--11:14).
7) Seventh trumpet: Christ begins reign on earth; the Temple of God is opened and the ark of the covenant is seen beyond the veil; following are lightning, voices, thunderings, earthquake and a great hail (third woe) (11:15-19).

4. **The Fourth Vision: The Woman, the Man-Child, and Perse-cution by the Dragon** (Rev. 12:1--14:20)
Scene: "A woman clothed with the sun" and "a great red dragon" appear in heaven (12:1-4).
   1) Woman brings forth a man child to rule all nations; the child is protected and the woman flees to the wilderness (12:5, 6) >
   2) War in heaven: Michael and his angels fight the dragon (accuser, serpent, deceiver) and his angels, and the dragon is cast to the earth (12:7-12).
   3) Woman persecuted by dragon, but earth helps the woman (12:13-17).
   4) A beast arises out of the sea with power of the dragon and is worshipped (13:1-10).
   5) A beast arises out of the earth, a false prophet of the other beast, and deceives by miracles (13:11-18).
   6) Followers of the Lamb perceive Babylon already fallen, but the worshippers of the beast to "have no rest day nor night" (14:1-13).
   7) Son of man reaps the harvest of the earth and another angel gathers the vine (14:14-20).

New-born Understanding of Truth Resisted by the "Dragon"

5. **The Fifth Vision: The Seven Vials of Judgment Poured Out and the Destruction of Babylon** (Rev. 15:1--18:24).
Scene: Angels in heaven prepare to pour out vials (bowls) of plagues on those on the earth with the mark of the beast (15:1-8).
   1) First vial: earth men tormented with grievous malignant sores (16:1, 2).
   2) Second vial: sea pollution brings death (16:3).
   3) Third vial: rivers and springs become blood (16:4-7).
   4) Fourth vial: sun scorching hot (16:8, 9).
   5) Fifth vial: seat of the beast full of darkness (16:10, 11).
   6) Sixth vial: river Euphrates dries up and forces gather at Armageddon (16:12-16).
   7) Seventh vial: air agitated, thunder, lightning, hail (16:17-21), and the Babylonish Woman (carried by the beast "that was and is not"), symbol of the great city of Babylon, is destroyed (17:1--18:24).

False Conscious-ness Yields to Power of Truth

6. **The Sixth Vision: Triumph of the Word of God, Destruction of the Dragon, and the End of Evil** (Rev. 19:1--20:15)
Scene: Victory over all evil on earth assured with announce-ment of the coming marriage of the Lamb (19:1-10).
   1) Word of God, white horse rider, wars victoriously (19:11-16).

All Evil and "Dragon" Finally Destroyed

95

2) Fowls of heaven banquet on all flesh (19:17, 18).

3) White horse rider conquers beast and false prophet and casts them into lake of fire (destruction) (19:19-21).

4) Dragon cast into the bottomless pit (helpless) (20:1-3).

5) The saints, who did not worship the beast, reign with Christ in the first resurrection--the millennium (second death has no power over them) (20:4-6).

6) Dragon loosed after "1000 years" and deceives Gog and Magog to war against the saints; but fire from heaven devours Gog and Magog and casts the dragon itself into the lake of fire (dragon destroyed) (20:7-10).

7) Earth and heaven flee from before One on the throne and the dead are judged by the book of life in the last resurrection--the Day of Judgment [Day of the Lord], and death and hell itself cast into lake of fire [this is the second death](20:11-15).

Spiritual Consciousness Realized

7. **The Seventh Vision: The New Jerusalem--the Holy City-- The Lamb's Bride Appears** (Rev. 21:1--22:5)
Scene: A new heaven and a new earth and no more sea (21:1).

1) New Jerusalem appears as a bride (21:2).

2) Tabernacle of God is with men (21:3, 4).

3) All things new; water of life given freely (21:5-8).

4) Description of New Jerusalem, the Lamb's bride, as a city foursquare (21:9-21).

5) Temple of City is God and the Lamb (21:22).

6) City ever lighted and gates never shut (21:23-27).

7) Pure river proceeding out of throne of God and the Lamb, and a tree of life bearing twelve fruits, and no more curse (22:1-5).

Epilogue: Admonitions

D. **Epilogue: Seven-fold Admonition to Church** (Rev. 22:6-19)

1. Keep the sayings of the Revelation (22:6, 7).

2. Worship God, not the revelator (22:8, 9).

3. Seal not the sayings of the Revelation--the time is at hand [here, now] (22:10-13).

4. Keep the Commandments (22:14, 15).

5. Testify in the churches (22:16).

6. Partake of the water of life freely (22:17).

7. Do not add to nor subtract from the words of the Revelation (22:18, 19).

Benediction

E. **Benediction** "He which testifieth these things saith, Surely I come quickly" (Rev. 22:20. 21).

FROM PRIMITIVE CHRISTIANITY
TO THE DARK AGES
(circa A.D. 100 to 500)

"The whole inhabited world wherein dwell the churches of God--established through Jesus by those who have turned from so many myriads of evils--has evidence of the work of Jesus. The name Jesus still removes ecstasies from the minds of men, as well as demons and diseases. Moreover it creates a wonderful gentleness, and a dignity of character, a philanthropy, an uprightness, and a kindness, in those who do not pretend to be Christians . . . but accept really the word of God."

-Origen in "Against Celsus" c. A.D. 250

I. THE FIRST CENTURY
    A. Christianity at the End of the First Century — *Christianity*
        1. Within two generations, primitive Christianity began undergoing changes.
        2. The reasons were many
            a. The passing of those who had personally known Jesus.
            b. The growth of the church among the Gentiles who brought with them some aspects of the Greek mystery cults and added them to their new faith.
            c. The development of rival groups within the church.
            d. The diminishing of the power to heal, though it continued until the third century.
            e. The dimming of the eschatological hope (Parousia) interpreted as a personal return of Jesus to earth to do battle with evil and usher in the Kingdom of God.
            f. The human desire to make a "religion" out of Jesus' teachings.
    B. Judaism at the End of the First Century — *Judaism*
        1. The Dispersion of the Jews (the Diaspora) dates from the 6th century B.C. From that time there were three distinct divisions among the Jews:
            a. The Palestinian Jews.
            b. The Jews in Mesopotamia (Babylonia).
            c. The Jews in Egypt who fled there and spread from there to the whole Mediterranean world. These were the Greek-speaking Jews who in 285 B.C. translated the Old Testament into Greek (Septuagint) which became the Christian Scriptures.

2. It was to the synagogues of the Jews throughout the Roman Empire that the Christian message was first preached.

3. Although there were periods of persecution (brought on by rebellions) the attitude of the Romans toward the Jews was friendly through the middle of the first century.

Rebellions

4. A disastrous rebellion of the Jews in Palestine began in A.D. 66, and ended with the razing of Jerusalem and the destruction of the Temple in A.D. 70.

5. A later rebellion (132-135) was also stamped out and with it Jewish Christianity. After that, it was Gentile Christianity that was established in Jerusalem.

6. With these uprisings in Palestine (and similar abortive uprisings elsewhere in the empire) Jews everywhere were viewed with suspicion and treated with severity. Initially some of the Roman persecution of Christianity was the result of its being viewed as a sect of Judaism.

Roman Empire

C. **The Roman Empire at the Turn of the Century**

  1. Society was divided into pronounced classes.

    a. Aristocrats of wealth and position devoted to self-indulgence and pleasure.

    b. Intellectuals devoted to literature and philosophy.

    c. Common people who struggled for existence and led simple lives.

    d. Slaves, a vast multitude brought from conquests, who had no rights and were often treated brutally.

  2. Christians came from all classes but chiefly were common people and slaves. Until the middle of the second century there was very little following among intellectuals. Christian fellowships included all and granted equality within Christian groups.

Caesars

D. **Roman Emperors (Caesars) and Christianity**

  1. Augustus (27 B.C.--A.D. 14) Luke 2:l.

  2. Tiberius (A.D. 14-37) Luke 3:1.

  3. Claudius (41-54) Acts 18:2.

  4. Nero (54-68). Blamed Christians for disastrous fire in Rome A.D. 64; martyrdom of Christians.

  5. Vespasian (69-79). Completed war in Judea and destruction of Jerusalem.

  6. Domitian (81-96). Suspicious of Jews and Christians; some persecution.

  7. Hadrian (117-138). Put down Jewish rebellion.

  8. Marcus Aurelius (161-180). Active wholesale persecution of Christians.

E. **Rivals of Christianity**

  1. Greek mystery cults.

    a. Eleusis, Dionysus, Orpheus, Cybele-Attis, Mithras, etc.

b. Esoteric rites and initiations to gain gnosis; emotional in appeal; stressed personal relation with deity; rites included a dramatization of the god's career including his death and resurrection, and a sacred meal, the partaking of which enabled the worshipper to take on the nature of the god through eating the flesh of the sacred animal; democratic brotherhoods; promise of immortality. *(Greek Mystery Religions)*

c. In Mithraism particularly, morality was also stressed. Mithras, as mediator between light and darkness, imposed ethical demands.

2. Astral religions. *(Astral Religions)*
    a. Magic and private mysteries.
    b. Rooted in astrology, an invention of the Chaldeans of Babylon.
    c. Belief that movements of heavenly bodies influenced fate of man, hence horoscopes and predictions by soothsayers, etc.

3. Emperor worship. *(Emperor Worship)*
    a. State cult emphasized to strengthen the state.
    b. Abstract deities as symbols of greatness of state, e.g. Pax, Fortuna Publica, Roma.
    c. Deified the emperor as both a political and religious focus for emotions of people in Empire. Christian refusal to worship the emperor was considered not only sacrilege but treason.

4. Epicureanism and Stoicism.
    a. "Religions" of the intellectuals.
    b. Paul in Athens quotes Stoic philosophers (Acts 17:28).
    c. Logos or Word in John's Gospel expresses Stoic conception (John 1:1-18).
    d. Stoicism taught a good Providence; God the Father; all men brothers; Logos is divine Reason, the divine spark in all to which we can remain true as we master passions and live rationally. *(Stoicism)*
    e. Epicureanism was hedonistic, taught that pleasure was the end of all morality. *(Epicureanism)*

5. Neo-Platonism (somewhat later). *(Neo-Platonism)*
    a. Eclectic, but sources in Plato's mysticism, transmuted by Oriental influences.
    b. Chief exponent was Plotinus (203-270), an Egyptian who taught in Rome.
    c. Some later influence on Christianity through such individuals as Augustine.

II. SECOND AND THIRD CENTURIES

A. Second Century Modifications of Primitive Christianity

Development
of Ritual

1. By the second century, the common meal (<u>agape</u>) had been discontinued and the Eucharist ritualized as part of the Sunday service. This ritualization was influenced by the rites of the Greek mystery cults. In two more centuries it had become the Mass and a priesthood developed.

2. Admission to membership was formalized by a course of instruction and testing, followed by baptism, the laying on of hands, anointing with oil, and the sign of the cross as a vow to give up old gods and old morality and follow the Christ. Baptism also now included infants (and even the dead by proxy). Confirmation followed instruction.

Authority of
Bishops

3. Authority of the boards of elders was more and more assumed by the bishops. By the end of the second century, a single bishop was in charge of each congregation, and the prophets, teachers and evangelists gradually disappeared from the scene. Leadership was no longer charismatic but appointed. As the bishops assumed spiritual authority, they began to develop a system of doctrine declared to be orthodox and an ecclesiastical organization.

Healing

4. Healing continued, though in diminished volume, through the second century, but after the opening of the third century dwindled rapidly. Evidence of such healing in the writings of Justin Martyr (<u>Second Apology</u>), Irenaeus (<u>Against Heresies</u>), Tatian (<u>Address to the Greeks</u>), and Origen in the third century (<u>Against Celsus</u>); also in the writings of Melito, Tertullian, Clement, Dionysius, Thaumaturges, Lactantius.

New Testament

B. Formation of the New Testament

1. Paul's letters had been read and re-read in the churches to which they were sent and shared with other churches. About A.D. 90 the letters were collected, and copies of the entire collection began to be circulated among the churches.

2. The Gospels were also written for particular groups and to be read in churches, and came to be shared with other groups. Sometime after the fourth Gospel appeared (<u>John</u>), it was combined with the other three as the fourfold Gospel and circulated as a unit, probably about A.D. 125. At this time <u>Luke</u> was separated from Luke's great book, <u>Luke-Acts</u>.

Canon

3. Canonization may be said to begin with Marcion whose list (A.D. 144) included Luke and ten letters of Paul. About A.D. 200, another list shows the fourfold Gospel, <u>Acts</u>, 13 Pauline letters, <u>Jude</u>, <u>I John</u>, <u>II John</u>, and the <u>Revelation</u> (with the comment "which some reject"). Also by the end of the second century the books were referred to as the New Testament.

4. Origen (c. 250) listed 29 books, the present 27 plus the letter to <u>Barnabas</u> and the <u>Shepherd of Hermas</u> (an apocalypse). He listed these two as "disputed" along with <u>James</u>, <u>II Peter</u>, <u>II John</u>, <u>III John</u>, and <u>Jude</u>. Eusebius in his <u>Church History</u> (c. 325) also lists these as disputed.

Origen

5. In 367, Athanasius, bishop of Alexandria, in a letter to his churches, enumerated 27 books we now have and this list Jerome used for the Vulgate Latin translation. Officially declared canon at Council of Carthage A.D. 397.

Canon

C. Early Doctrinal Disputes and Heresies

1. Docetism.

   Docetism

   a. Belief: Jesus had not a real, but merely an apparent body. He only <u>seemed</u> to suffer, die and rise again.

   b. Develops early in the churches.

2. Marcionism.

   Marcionism

   a. Belief: Impossible to reconcile concepts of God in Old Testament and New Testament (refused to use allegory), therefore there must be two gods: the Old Testament God, inferior, sometimes cruel, emphasizing justice; the New Testament God, superior, free from Old Testament Law, emphasizing love.

   b. Marcion sought to restore "original" New Testament text, to remove "Judaizing interpolations".

   c. Marcion emphasized asceticism.

   d. Flourished until the fourth century. Many martyrs.

3. Gnosticism.

   Gnosticism

   a. Gnosis--revealed knowledge--the way back to good. Constantly evolving, combining elements of Judaism, Oriental philosophy, mystery religions, magic and astrology in cosmological and theological speculations.

   b. Belief: Dualistic (Zoroastrian influence). Two opposing worlds: (1) a spiritual universe, light, good, incorruptible, and (2) a material world, dark, inherently evil, corruptible. Since (1) cannot be source of (2), a number of intermediaries deemed necessary ("thrones, powers," etc. referred to in Colossians) to bring the two together. Demiurge (creator of the world) sometimes considered evil, sometimes as emanation from God trying to bring order into material chaos.

   c. Manichaean Christians and other semi-gnostic groups flourished into fourth century. Many martyrs.

   d. In rejecting the heresy of Gnosticism (the theosophical intermediaries theory), the Church also rejected the early Christian teaching that matter (flesh) is evil and not the creation of God, thus adopting the dogma that God is the creator of both matter and Spirit.

D. Development of Creeds

Apostles' Creed

1. The so-called "Apostles' Creed" was developed late in the second century as a statement of Christian belief against the rival Gnostics, Marcionites and others. Its earliest form in A.D. 150-175.

E. Persecutions

Persecution of Christians

1. By the end of the second century, persecution (being thrown to the lions or burned at the stake) began and sporadically continued to the fourth century.

2. In the middle of the third century, the Emperor Decius demanded that every citizen of the Roman Empire get a certificate from a government official affirming that he sacrificed to the image of the emperor. Failure to do so meant death. Multitudes of Christians refused to yield.

3. At the beginning of the fourth century, Emperor Diocletian decreed that all Christian churches be destroyed, the Scriptures confiscated, and clergy and congregations tortured until they sacrificed to the emperor's image.

Causes of Persecution

4. Main causes of persecutions:

   a. Judaism, some Greek mystery cults, were legally recognized but Christianity was not, and so open to public persecution.

   b. Christianity, unlike other religions of empire (except specially privileged Judaism) refused recognition to other gods, including emperor; therefore was considered dangerous to the state.

   c. Christians socially exclusive; would not eat meat sacrificed to idols, so rarely ate with pagans; sometimes refused to hold civic office or serve in army, because this necessitated divided allegiance.

   d. Popular misconceptions, charges of atheism, infant sacrifice, cannibalism, "secret" meetings, etc.

   e. Rome was troubled by civil wars, barbarian invasions, plagues, all signs of the gods' anger; Christians were useful scapegoats.

5. Vast underground catacombs of Rome, used by Christians for refuge, worship and burial during persecutions.

F. Influential Church Leaders

Early Leaders

1. Polycarp (69-156) of Smyrna, pupil of John.

2. Ignatius (67-110) of Antioch, pupil of John.

3. Clement (?-101) of Rome.

4. Marcion (85-160) of Asia Minor and Rome.

5. Papias (70-160) of Hierapolis, church historian.

6. Justin Martyr (100-167) of Neapolis (Nablus).

7. Irenaeus (130-200) of Lyons, pupil of Polycarp.

8. Clement (150-215) of Alexandria.

9. Tertullian (160-220) of Carthage.

   a. Doctrinal disputations between Clement and Tertullian.   **Disputes**

   b. By 200 two theologies, two different eschatologies, two understandings of the Trinity, and even two ethics divided East and West.

10. Origen (185-254) of Caesarea.   **Origen**

   a. Greatest teacher between Paul and Augustine. For a century after his death all leading Greek-speaking churchmen were his disciples.

   b. Prolific writer and Bible scholar, sought inspired meaning of the Bible through allegory.

11. Eusebius (264-340) of Caesarea, church historian.   **Eusebius**

III. FOURTH AND FIFTH CENTURIES

A. Constantine   **Constantine**

1. In 323 persecutions abruptly ended after Constantine became Roman emperor. Although not yet a Christian, he was sympathetic. He declared Sunday a legal holiday, gave Christianity equality with other religions, and even personally called and presided at a conference of bishops at Nicea to decide a controversy as to the nature of Christ!

2. Forty years after Constantine, Christianity was made the only official religion of the Roman Empire (A.D. 383).

3. Pagan festivals and celebrations gradually modified and adapted to become Christian holidays: Easter, Christmas, etc.

B. Further Creedal Development

1. The Nicene Creed (A.D. 325).   **Nicene Creed**

   a. Expansion of the Apostles' Creed; developed as a statement against the teachings of Arius.

   b. Arius, a presbyter of Alexandria (deposed in 321), denied that Jesus was God. His opponent was his bishop at Alexandria, Athanasius.

   c. At the Nicene Council, presided over by Constantine, the Athanasian view prevailed with the 300 bishops, and the Arian view was declared heretical.

   d. Arian Christians then carried their version of Christianity to heathens outside the empire.

2. The Creed of Chalcedon (A.D. 451).   **Creed of Chalcedon**

   a. Creed opposed teachings of Nestorius (381-451), bishop of Constantinople; opponent Cyril of Alexandria.

   b. Nestorius preached against calling the Virgin Mary, "the mother of God" for she did not bear God, but "a man, the organ of deity". He attempted to make a distinction between the divine Christ and the human Jesus.

   c. The Nestorian Christians were banished; went to Syria, Persia, India, and eventually China.

Monasticism

C. Rise of Monasticism

1. A response to lack of spirituality in Christians-in-name-only, increasingly complex creeds and doctrinal beliefs, and the idea that acceptance of creed was more important to spirituality than reformation of worldly thought and action.
2. The new movement felt that by asceticism and renouncing the world, one could achieve spirituality.
3. Began in the third century and continued to grow until it came to be regarded as <u>the</u> religious life.
4. A positive result: in the monasteries, learning was kept alive as monks copied and preserved manuscripts and books.

Augustine

D. Augustine (354-430)

1. Bishop of Hippo in North Africa, a learned convert to Christianity after a dissolute youth; great theologian, his doctrines and teaching on grace, predestination, original sin, etc. helped shape the Middle Ages and later the Protestant Reformation.
2. Opposed to Augustine's doctrine of original sin, a monk, Pelagius, taught that each has spiritual capacity to choose between good and evil. Pelagianism declared heresy in 431.

Jerome

E. Jerome (c. 347-420)

1. A leading scholar appointed by Damasus, bishop of Rome, to make an official Latin Version of the Bible to replace various Old Latin translations. Completed A.D. 405.
2. His monumental translation, known as the "Vulgate" (common), was for 1,000 years, up to the time of the Reformation, the chief Bible of the Christian World.

Fall of Rome

F. Fall of Rome

1. The far-flung Roman Empire was being attacked by a variety of invaders (Visigoths, Ostrogoths, Bergundians, Vandals, and Lombards) from about A.D. 200.
2. By the fifth century the invaders succeeded in plundering Rome, A.D. 455, and the Western Roman empire fell. (The Eastern Byzantine Empire lasted another thousand years).
3. The invaders were Arian Christians so they did not disturb the Roman churches.

Rise of Papacy

G. Rise of the Papacy

1. For some time the Church at Rome had declared its special importance.
2. In the late fourth century the bishops of Constantinople, Antioch, Rome, Jerusalem, and Alexandria were offered the title of "Patriarch" but the bishop of Rome refused the title saying his title was "pope" ("father" in English).
3. By the end of the fifth century the pope in Rome declared his primacy over all other bishops, and the primacy of the Church of Rome over all other churches.

FROM THE DARK AGES
TO THE MIDDLE AGES
(circa A.D. 500 to 1000)

"Hail to Charles the Augustus, crowned by God the great and peace-bringing Emperor of the Romans."   -Pope Leo III, A.D. 800
on crowning Charlemagne

I. EMERGENCE FROM THE DARK AGES
A. The Dark Ages
   1. The period following the fall of the Roman Empire is called the Dark Ages (roughly 500 to 800).
   2. On the ruins of the Roman Empire, the Roman Church filled the power vacuum, proved to be the most stable institution in a shattering society.

`Dark Ages`

B. The Threat of Islam
   1. In Arabia a new prophet, Mohammed (570-632) began teaching a monotheism (his book: the Koran). Arabs swept east to India and west to France, subjugated Persia, Egypt and Spain. Within 100 years, they won an empire bigger than the one the Romans had built up in 600 years and they commanded the world's trade routes from Canton to Cordova. Finally turned back in France in the 8th century.
   2. By A.D. 1000, Moslem culture reached a peak with translation of Plato and Aristotle into Arabic; great universities were established at Cordova (Spain) and Baghdad; from Cordova the work of Aristotle was brought to Christian monks.
   3. Moors (Moslems) not finally driven from Spain until 1492.

`Islam`

C. Increasing Papal Power and Decadence
   1. The Bishop of Rome assumed increasing political authority and the papacy increased in power and influence.
   2. In 800 A.D. Charlemagne was crowned emperor of the "Holy Roman Empire" by the pope in an attempt by the Church to restore the lost empire. Charlemagne conquered most of Western Europe and for two decades there was comparative peace.
   3. A period of political disintegration followed with much corruption in the church. The "Holy Roman Empire" continued breaking into national states.

`Charlemagne`

4. Era of what has been called "pornocracy" in papacy. Marozia, mistress of Pope Sergius III becomes mother of Pope John XI, aunt of John XIII, and grandmother of Benedict VI.

Church-State Struggle

5. Struggle between church and state increased in intensity for the practice of deeding land to the church to gain benefits after death had resulted in church ownership of nearly one-third of France and similarly large areas of Italy and Germany. The Church was the largest Feudal landlord in Europe.

6. Religiously the Church of Jesus which held the key to life had become the Church of Rome which held the keys to death. The next life, not this, was the central religious concern of the Church, which was regarded as the earthly representative of a heavenly St. Peter determining reward and punishment and granting indulgences.

Empire Breaks

II. THE EASTERN CHURCH
A. Roman Empire Breaks in Two
1. With the crowning of Charlemagne, the political break between East and West made official. The eastern Byzantine Empire continued until finally falling to the Turks in 1453.

Church East West Split

B. Western and Eastern Church Split
1. Jurisdictional and doctrinal disputes between the Roman Church and the Eastern Church began early and continued for over 300 years. The final and complete break came in 1054.
2. Permanent introduction of sacred pictures (icons) into the churches of Constantinople in 842 settled an age-long controversy over the issue of icons.

Slavs

C. Conversion of Slavs
1. Monk Methodius converted Bulgarian prince Bogoris, and thus the Bulgarians. Conversions of princes of Moravia, Bohemia, and Poland and their peoples to Eastern Christianity followed in the early 900s.
2. Russian prince Vladimir of Kiev sent emissaries to Poland to investigate Christianity and brought missionaries back to Kiev. Ordered all his people to be baptized into the Eastern Church (988).
3. Ultimately the Western Church wrested Moravia, Bohemia and Poland from the Eastern Church and converted the populations to Roman Christian control and forms.

Formation of Eastern Orthodox Church

D. Eastern Orthodoxy
1. Eastern Orthodoxy rejected the idea of a "pope". Churches were led by patriarchs who more or less corresponded to national boundaries (Greek Orthodox, Russian Orthodox, etc.), though essentially united in doctrine.

FROM THE MIDDLE AGES
TO THE REFORMATION
(circa A.D. 1000 to 1500)

"If, then, there be anyone who, boastfully taking pride in his supposed wisdom, wishes to challenge what we have written, let him not do it in some corner, nor before children who are powerless to decide such difficult matters. Let him reply openly if he dare. He shall find me here confronting him, and not only my negligible self, but many another whose study is truth. We shall do battle with his errors, and bring a cure to his ignorance."

-Thomas Aquinas, A.D. 1270

I. ROMAN CHURCH SUPREME IN THE WEST
A. Struggle for Power
1. As feudalism grew, popes struggled with monarchs over the question of whether kings were subject to the head of the Church. | Papal Power
   a. Climax when Pope Gregory VII forced King Henry IV of Germany to stand for three successive days in the snow, barefoot and clad in penitent's garb beseeching the pope to lift his excommunication.
2. By the end of the 12th Century, papal power was unquestioned. Rulers did the bidding of the pope. The Church claimed supreme jurisdiction in all matters.
3. The life of the common man revolved completely around the Church, unquestioning her power and authority.
B. Great Cathedrals Built

II. THE MIDDLE AGES
A. The Crusades | Crusades
1. For two hundred years, Crusades were organized to win back the Holy Land from Islam.
2. The fanatical Crusaders not only took on Islam but Orthodox Christians at Constantinople as well, leading to the downfall of that city to the Turks in 1453.
B. Medieval Monasticism | Monasticism
1. Dominic of Spain (1170-1221).
2. Francis of Assissi, Italy (1182-1226).
3. Bernard of Clairvaux, France (1090-1153).

C. Scholasticism

1. From Spain came Arabic texts of Aristotle's writings studied at the University of Cordova--a systematic treatment of natural science.
2. Study of these texts, by church schoolmen resulted in a "new theology", a reconciliation of faith and philosophy by Thomas Aquinas--combining Aristotle with Christian revelation. Dogmatic from beginning to end, but flexible. Granted theology the highest place but gave humanism and naturalism also roles to play.

D. Medieval Literature

1. Dante Alighieri, <u>Divine Comedy</u>.

E. Medieval Mysticism

1. Refusal to believe that direct vision had to await passage to the next world.
2. One product: <u>Imitation of Christ</u>, by Thomas a Kempis.

III. DECLINE OF THE PAPACY

A. Twelfth Century Protests

1. Reactions to the temporal power, wealth, and materialism of the Church.

2. The Cathari (also called the Albigenses) in Southern Europe.
   a. Dualistic: good god (Spirit) evil god (matter); struggle between forces; goal: purification from matter.
   b. Cathari destroyed. A Crusade in the south of France destroyed great numbers, and finally the Inquisition, through various forms of mental and physical torture.

3. The Waldenses in Western Europe.
   a. Named for Peter Waldo, merchant of Lyons.
   b. Translated New Testament, and made an effort to live in simplicity of early church. Despite excommunication, movement persisted for several centuries before allying itself to the Reformation.

B. A Weakened Papacy

1. Church forbids Bible reading by all laymen in 1229.
2. After the 13th century national kings increasingly asserted their independence from the papacy.

3. In 1309 the papacy was removed from Rome to Avignon in France and was made a French institution.
4. At one time, there were as many as three popes, all claiming title. Not until 1417 was a single papacy restored to Rome.

C. Rise of the Universities

1. In the 11th century, universities (as associations of teachers and students) were organized in Paris, Oxford, and Bologna.
2. By 1500 there were 72 universities in Europe.

3. With learning came questioning, and with questioning came heresy, and with heresy came the Inquisition, a brutal method to counteract "treason against God".

4. Among the early reformers deemed "heretics":

    a. John Wyclif [Wycliffe] (1320-1384), professor at Oxford, England. Reformer, Bible translator, influential writer, condemned a heretic. Followers: Lollards.

    b. John Huss (1369-1415), rector of University of Prague. Burned at stake. Followers: Hussites.

    c. Girolamo Savonarola (1452-1498), Dominican preacher in Florence. Reformer. Hanged.

D. Rise of the Common Man

1. Rise of self-government with the appearance of the merchant class or middle class after an absence of a thousand years. They demanded their wishes be heard by the noblemen and bishops.

2. Signing of Magna Carta in England (1215) and organization of "Mother of Parliaments".

3. Beginnings of parliaments in France, Germany, Sweden, Denmark, Switzerland, Holland.

4. With growth of towns and cities and increase in middle class, commoners demanded more power, and power of feudal rulers decreased.

E. The Renaissance

1. The fall of Constantinople in the 15th century brought many scholars fleeing to Italy with the literary masterpieces of the ancient Greeks in the original tongue. Thus began the revival of classical learning known as the Renaissance.

2. The revival of learning fostered an appreciation of man and the present life in place of the contemplation of a future heaven and hell.

3. Painters, sculptors, and writers flourished: Leonardo da Vinci, Michelangelo, Raphael, Machiavelli, etc.

4. North of the Alps another awakening, usually termed "humanism" flourished through the tongue and pen of the Dutch scholar Erasmus (1466-1536). His specially edited Greek New Testament (1516), rendered from Greek codices released after sacking of Constantinople by the Turks in 1453, was basis for later translators including Tyndale and Luther.

F. Invention of Printing

1. The invention of printing in 1454 enabled the new ideas to spread rapidly.

2. The first book printed with movable type by Johannes Gutenberg--the Bible.

Margin notes: "Heretics" · Rise of Self-government · Renaissance · Invention of Printing

"Here I stand."

MARTIN LUTHER

FROM THE REFORMATION
TO OUR OWN TIME
(circa A.D. 1500 to date)

"Prove me out of Scripture that I am wrong, and I submit. . . . Here I stand. I can do no otherwise; so help me God! Amen!"

-Martin Luther, 1521

I. RIPE FOR THE REFORMATION
A. Climate at the Beginning of the 16th Century
1. Curiosity about the Bible, particularly in northern Europe.
2. Questioning of such church practices as sale of indulgences, obligatory confession, papal taxation, etc.
3. Rising influence of the middle class which had gained experience in government.
4. Movement toward individualism, freedom, and democracy.
5. Age of explorers (Columbus, Magellan, Balboa, etc.).
6. The Church appeared increasingly as a vast system of financial exactions, luxury, materialism, irreverence, and corruption. All attempts at reform had failed.
7. The Church seemed left behind by progress, trapped in cramping institutionalism, conservatism, and conformity.

Climate for Reformation

B. Martin Luther (1483-1546) in Germany
1. An Augustinian monk, ordained to priesthood in 1507, later appointed professor of theology at the University of Wittenberg. Considered "father of the Reformation".
2. Came to conviction that salvation was by faith alone, the Bible was the only authority, and all believers were priests.
3. On October 31, 1517, Luther tacked 97 theses to the door of the Wittenberg church for the purpose of sparking debate on the sale of indulgences.
4. Luther excommunicated in 1520.
5. Luther translated the New Testament into German, and later the Old Testament.
6. Phillip Melanchthon, an able assistant of Luther, wrote first handbook of Lutheran theology.

Martin Luther

C. Ulrich Zwingli (1484-1531) in Zurich, Switzerland
1. A more radical reformation than Luther's. In Switzerland the forces of humanism, local self-government, and extreme dislike of ecclesiastical authority were strong.

Ulrich Zwingli

Zwingli

2. Zwingli, a parish priest in German-speaking Switzerland, began work in 1522, removed all images and crosses, discontinued celebration of the Mass, eliminated ritual, and turned church government over to elders.

3. Zwingli fell in one of the battles of the civil war between Catholic and Reformed forces.

John Calvin

D. John Calvin (1509-1564) in Geneva, Switzerland

1. A young French scholar, an exile from France, published <u>The Institutes of the Christian Religion</u> at age 26; became leader of Swiss reformation, and is called "the second father of the Reformation".

2. Calvinistic theology greatly influenced the West. From it grew the "Protestant Ethic" with emphasis on duty, industry, thrift, work, and self-discipline. Became theme of Puritans.

3. Succeeded in Geneva by Theodore Beza (1519-1605).

E. Reformation in France and the Low Countries

Huguenots

1. Calvinism spread to France and the French Protestants (Huguenots) under the leadership of Admiral Coligny were bitterly fought by the Catholic clergy and French court.

2. In the Massacre of St. Bartholomew in August, 1572, 20,000 Protestants were slaughtered at one time.

3. In 1598 Protestants won toleration though 100 years later it was again denied by France.

4. Bitter struggle in Low Countries, then under Spanish control. When finally able to throw off Spain, Holland became a Calvinistic land with Reformed churches.

John Knox

F. John Knox (1505-1572) in Scotland

1. John Knox, a disciple of Calvin in Geneva, upon his return to Scotland founded the Church of Scotland (Presbyterian Church).

2. Dramatic confrontation between Knox and Catholic Mary, Queen of the Scots, but Scotland remained Protestant.

G. Reformation in England

1. England had no Calvin, Knox, or Luther.

2. Wyclif, in the 14th century, and his followers, the Lollards, labored for reform through translation and circulation of the Bible in English.

3. Efforts continued by other translators of the Bible: Tyndale (burnt at stake 1536), Coverdale, and Whittingham.

King Henry VIII

4. King Henry VIII broke with the Church of Rome, but favored no changes in religious doctrine. His only concession was to allow the Bible in English in the churches.

5. Catholic Queen Mary (Bloody Mary) opposed Protestants. She deposed and burnt as a heretic archbishop Thomas Cranmer in 1556. Her successor was Protestant Queen Elizabeth.

6. Queen Elizabeth promoted Protestantism--the Church of England (Anglican or Episcopal)--and authorized the <u>Book of Common Prayer</u> in 1559. However, she took steps to stamp out the Puritans who sought reform of the Church.

Queen Elizabeth

H. Counter-Reformation

Counter-Reformation

1. Protestant Reformation resulted in a church-wide call within the Roman Catholic Church for reform.
2. Pressure upon Pope Paul III to call the Council of Trent in 1545. The Council met over a period of eighteen years.
3. Result of Council:
   a. A re-statement of Catholic dogma that made any reconciliation with the Protestants impossible.
   b. A church-wide Inquisition was re-organized to operate wherever a favorable government would allow it, to purge the Protestants. The first country thus cleared was Italy.

Inquisition

   c. New religious orders were established; the most important was the Jesuit Order (Society of Jesus) founded by Ignatius Loyola. Marked by rigid military-like discipline, "spiritual exercises" to discipline the individual will, and absolute obedience to superiors, sanctioning even "mental reservation" in the case of not being required to tell the whole truth under oath. Purpose: to destroy Protestantism.

Jesuit Order

   d. Stricter regulation of indulgences and of veneration of the saints was adopted.
   e. An Index of forbidden books (Protestant writings).

Index

I. Other Reformation Movements

1. <u>Anabaptists</u> arose in Switzerland, particularly emphasizing adult baptism. Later called Mennonites. Persecuted both by Protestants and Catholics.

Anabaptists

2. <u>Unitarians</u> in Hungary denied the Trinity as it was defined by Protestant and Catholic Churches. Followers of Socinus (or Sozzini) and influenced by the writings of Michael Servetus (1511-1553), who was burned at the stake. Persecuted by both Catholic Inquisition and Protestants. Fled from one country to another, then to Holland and later to New England, as a liberal movement within the Congregational Church before breaking away.

Unitarians

II. LATER DEVELOPMENTS

A. The Puritans and Other Non-Conformist Groups

Puritans

1. Nonconformists within the Church of England, largely Calvinist in doctrine, desired to purify the Church of England of its "Romish" elements. These Puritans were subject to periodic persecution and harshness.

Puritans

King James
Version

Pilgrims

Quakers

Pietists

Age of Science

Deism

2. Puritans at times, however, reached considerable power in England.

3. When King James I came to the throne, he agreed to the request of the Puritans that a new translation of the Bible be prepared. It was issued in 1611, the familiar King James Version or Authorized Version (contemporary with William Shakespeare).

4. Somewhat later in the 17th Century, nonconformists were forced out of the English Anglican Church to become Congregationalists, Baptists, Quakers, Unitarians, Presbyterians, [emphases: congregational government, Bible base, prayer].

5. John Milton's <u>Paradise Lost</u> and John Bunyan's <u>The Pilgrim's Progress</u>.

6. Earlier fleeing Puritans (the Pilgrims) went to Holland under the leadership of John Robinson. Part of the group went to America in 1620 on the Mayflower. More Puritans arrived later, claiming New England for the Congregational Church.

7. Baptists [emphasis: adult baptism] came to Rhode Island.

8. Quakers (Society of Friends) came to Pennsylvania. Founded by George Fox (1624-1691) in England. Friends rejected all ritual and professional ministry; each member guided by the "inner light".

9. A group in Germany calling themselves "a church within a church" developed in Lutheranism. Pietists devoted themselves to Bible study and prayer, and eventually separated to become the Moravian Brethren.

B. Deism and the Enlightenment

1. Modern age of science began in the 16th and 17th centuries. Despite bitter opposition from the Church, men like Copernicus, Galileo, and Newton arrived at new explanations of natural phenomena.

2. By the 18th century, the development of science, the rise of capitalism, and world exploration and discoveries, created the period known as the Enlightenment or the Age of Reason.

3. Religion now compelled to justify its case before empirically-minded men. The educated abandoned what they regarded as religious dogma.

4. Most of the highly educated in England and the Continent became Deists. Many of the clergy of the Church of England also. Likewise the American founding fathers such as Thomas Jefferson, George Washington, Benjamin Franklin, John Adams, and Thomas Paine.

5. Deism avoided the clash between science and religion by separating God from His creation, conceiving that the creation ran by itself (a mechanism), and could therefore be a separate object of study.

C. The Methodists--John Wesley (1703-1791)

    1. A response to the influence of Deism.

    2. John Wesley and his associates sought to bring spiritual revival, emotional fire and conviction to the Anglican (Episcopal) Church of England.

    3. Called "methodists" because Wesley's "Holy Club" at Oxford met regularly for methodical study and prayer, endeavoring to find God for themselves. Key was "conversion".

    4. Sought to reform church from within, but soon separated.

    5. Spread to American colonies and across the Alleghenies into the vast spaces of the Middle West as a result of the efforts of such great "circuit riders" as Francis Asbury.

D. Religion in America

    1. The immigrants with each new wave brought their own religions with them. Before long, every church of Europe was represented in America.

    2. A few groups [such as Seventh Day Adventists (William Miller, Ellen G. White), Church of God, Disciples of Christ (Alexander Campbell), Universalist, Evangelical United Brethren, Pentecostal groups such as Assembly of God, etc.] developed in America, usually offshoots of or divisions within existing churches. Three distinctive groups originated in America which have spread around the world: the Jehovah's Witnesses (C. T. Russell), the Mormons (Church of Jesus Christ of Latter Day Saints founded by Joseph Smith and later led by Brigham Young) and the Christian Scientists (Church of Christ, Scientist, founded by Mary Baker Eddy).

E. Church and State in America

    1. At first, American colonies accepted European pattern of union of church and state. Nine of thirteen colonies had state churches.

    2. In Rhode Island (purchased from the Indians by Baptist Roger Williams), Pennsylvania (a Quaker state founded by William Penn), and Maryland (where the Catholic proprietor had to assure toleration to satisfy a Protestant King and Parliament) the conception of establishment first challenged.

    3. By 1776, there was a fast-growing conviction that a church establishment was a prolific source of political as well as religious evils.

    4. Virginia's "Declaration of Rights" adopted a few weeks before the Declaration of Independence, asserted that "all men are equally entitled to the free exercise of religion".

    5. A decade later Virginia's "Act for establishing Religious Freedom" (written by Jefferson) denied the right of the state to levy taxes for the support of a church or to require church membership as a test of eligibility for public office.

Margin notes: John Wesley · Methodists · New Groups · Church and State · Religious Freedom

115

First Amendment

6. Adoption of the first amendment of the U.S. Constitution, "Congress shall make no law respecting an establishment of religion" gave legal status to the principle of separation of church and state throughout America.

7. For the first time since 383 A.D. the Christian Church was again a voluntary association.

III. NINETEENTH AND TWENTIETH CENTURIES
A. Nineteenth Century

Movements

1. English born movements spread across America: YMCA, Salvation Army (William Booth), Sunday School movement (organized in 1780 by Robert Raikes), missionary movement, Bible societies, social gospel (Walter Rauschenbusch), etc.

2. Confrontation between religious modernists and fundamentalists was ignited by Darwin's theory of evolution and questions raised by modern Bible scholarship. The confrontation continues to this day.

Transcendentalism

3. New England Transcendentalism, began in the Unitarian fold of William Ellery Channing; exponents included Ralph Waldo Emerson, Bronson Alcott, Theodore Parker, Henry David Thoreau, James Russell Lowell, and William Lloyd Garrison. Leading ideas: supremacy of mind over matter, greater spirituality of woman, innate wisdom of children, perfectibility of man, equality of all men. Provided seedbed for abolitionist movement.

Pragmatism

4. Pragmatism under intellectual leadership of William James (rather than New England transcendentalism) became America's philosophy: faith in scientific method, in experiment, in Darwinian progress, in adaptation to changing environment, in empirical values and concrete results.

5. While transcendentalism and pragmatism occupied the intellectuals, two new-old ideas engaged the attention of the ordinary New Englander--spiritualism and mesmerism (hypnotism). A synthesis, growing out of spiritualism and combined with Oriental religious philosophy and esoteric mysticism, bore the name of theosophy. Other such syntheses in many variations continue to this day under such names as new thought, positive thinking, mind over matter, mind power, and a host of "New Age" religions and psychologies.

Mary Baker
Eddy

6. It was in an atmosphere of religious unrest and questioning within and without religious folds in New England that Mary Baker Eddy, in 1866, discovered Christian Science. The Church of Christ, Scientist, founded in 1879 was, in her words, "designed to commemorate the words and works of our Master which should reinstate primitive Christianity and its lost element of healing."

7. Christian Science, Mary Baker Eddy maintained, came from spiritual illumination, deep and consecrated study of the Bible, and her own religious experience--"through revelation, reason, and demonstration". Her statement of her discovery is in her book, <u>Science and Health with Key to the Scriptures</u>, first published in 1875, and subsequently revised by its author. Predictably a <u>woman</u> in the nineteenth century challenging science, theology and medicine engendered intense ridicule and opposition and no welcome from traditional churches.

Science and Health with Key to the Scriptures

B. Twentieth Century

Twentieth Century Developments and Change

1. Characterized by accelerating technological change (including robotics and computerization), man's increasing mastery of (and damage to) the physical environment, and a host of social, economic, political, ethical and human survival issues and problems.

2. Continuing advance toward the ideal of equality and human rights in a world plagued by poverty, social injustice, prejudice, discrimination and oppression.

3. Continuing advance toward the ideal of a world community as the alternative to the threat of annihilation in global war.

4. Continuing changes in medicine, research in biophysics, biochemistry, and psychosomatic medicine pointing to a mind-matter continuum; new practices in psychotherapy and new understandings of mental causation of disease.

Medicine

5. Continuing changes in theology with re-definitions of God, Christ, heaven, hell, the nature of man, the role of religion in life, the role of the clergy, and attention to spiritual healing in some denominations and in charismatic groups.

Theology

6. Continuing changes in science--from the 19th century belief in rigid and immutable matter to the equation of matter with energy; acceptance of the relativity theory and the "principle of uncertainty" and new physics.

Science

7. The revolution and reformation in Roman Catholicism triggered by Pope John XXIII, bringing the Roman church into the 20th century and closer to mainstream Protestantism.

Church

8. The challenges to "mainstream" Christianity of materialism, logical empiricism, agnosticism, secularism, atheism, as well as pentecostalism, fundamentalism, harmonialism, and "new age religions".

9. The church-wide searching throughout Christendom, and ecumenical merger efforts to end the fragmented church.

10. Continuing force of Bible scholarship and the development of clearer understanding and more accurate translation of the Scriptures.

Bible Scholarship

THE GOSPEL ACCORDING TO YOU

If none but you in the world today
Had tried to live in a Christ-like way,
Could the rest of the world look close at you
And find the path that is straight and true?

If none but you in the world so wide
Had found the Christ for his daily guide,
Would the things you do and the things you say
Lead others to live in His blessed way?

Ah, friends of the Christ, in the world today
Are many who watch you upon your way,
And look to the things you say and do
To measure the Christian standard true.

Men read and admire the Gospel of Christ
With its love so unfailing and true,
But what do they say and what do they think
Of the Gospel according to you?

You are writing each day a letter to men--
Take care that the writing is true;
'Tis the only Gospel that some men will read,
That Gospel according to you.

                                        - Anonymous

APPENDIX I

BIBLE STUDY AIDS

Bibles
Translations
Concordances
Dictionaries
Commentaries
Study Helps

"They received the word with all readiness of mind, and searched the Scriptures daily, whether these things were so." -Acts 17:11

KING JAMES VERSION REFERENCE BIBLES

Indispensable for the Bible student is a <u>Reference Bible</u> containing a cross-reference system that enables the reader to link verses being studied to other citations in the Scriptures. References to related citations may appear in a center column, as footnotes, or following each verse, depending on the edition. Editions usually also include a brief concordance and/or dictionary, maps, and a list of KJV words that have changed in meaning.

The **KING JAMES VERSION** is available in reference editions in a variety of styles, sizes and bindings from the following Bible publishers:

Cambridge University Press
Thomas Nelson Publishers
Holman Bible Publishers
Collins-World
American Bible Society

KING JAMES VERSION STUDY BIBLES

<u>Study Bibles</u> contain a cross-reference system similar to a Reference Bible, but in addition, include introductions to books, extensive explanatory notes and commentary, maps, essays, charts, book outlines, study aids, concise concordance and dictionary, and more, depending on the Bible. Study Bibles have a theological bias, typically in King James Study Bibles, a traditional, conservative and fundamentalist theological bias. Several study Bibles (KJV) are listed below:

<u>The Companion Bible</u> (E. W. Bullinger). Grand Rapids: Zondervan, reprinted 1974.
<u>The Open Bible</u>, KJV Expanded Edition. Nashville: Thomas Nelson, 1985.
<u>The New Thompson Chain Reference Bible</u>, KJV (F.C. Thompson). Indianapolis: B. B. Kirkbride, 1964.
<u>Dickson New Analytical Study Bible</u>, KJV. Iowa Falls: World Bible Publishers, 1973.
<u>The New Scofield Reference Bible</u>, KJV. London: Oxford University Press, 1967.
<u>Master Study Bible</u>, KJV. Nashville: Holman Bible Publishers, 1983.

Study Bibles are also available in a number of modern versions, e. g. New English, Revised Standard Version, New International, New King James, etc.

The Holy Bible: Revised Standard Version (American scholars; revision of the King James in contemporary language). Nashville: Thomas Nelson, 1952.

New Revised Standard Version (new revision of the Revised Standard Version based on oldest and most reliable texts). New York: Oxford University Press, 1989.

The New English Bible (British scholars, fresh and lively rendition from most ancient texts now available, fluent, clear, majestic literary style). New York: Oxford University Press, 1970.

The Revised English Bible (British scholars, major revision of the New English Bible). New York: Oxford University Press, 1989.

A New Translation of the Bible (James Moffatt; rendering by an eminent Bible scholar). New York: Harper and Row, 1934.

Good News Bible: The Bible in Today's English Version (clear translation for English-speaking people wherever English is spoken). New York: American Bible Society, 1976.

The Holy Bible: New International Version (International scholars; conservative alternative for RSV, known for idiomatic accuracy, fresh, contemporary). New York: International Bible Society, 1984.

New King James Version (updated King James modernizing archaic words, punctuation, but preserving cadence and rhythm). Nashville: Thomas Nelson, 1982.

The Bible, An American Translation (OT translated by J. M. Powis Smith and NT translated by Edgar J. Goodspeed). Chicago: University of Chicago Press, 1939.

New American Standard Bible (noted for word for word fidelity to the Hebrew and Greek). New York: Cambridge, 1971.

Bible in Basic English (simple English, vocabulary limited to 1000 words). New York: Cambridge, 1950.

The Modern Language Bible: The New Berkeley Version in Modern English (noted for competent scholarship and contemporary American language). Grand Rapids: Zondervan, 1969.

The Holy Bible from Ancient Eastern Manuscripts (George M. Lamsa; translation of Syriac Aramaic Peshitta text). Nashville: A. J. Holman, 1961.

The Jerusalem Bible (Roman Catholic scholars; acclaimed for clarity of meaning). Garden City, NY: Doubleday Co., 1966.

The New American Bible (official Roman Catholic modern language version). New York: Catholic Publishing Co., 1970.

The Amplified Bible (American scholars; includes clarifying shades of meaning conveyed by the original Hebrew and Greek words by amplification in the English text). Grand Rapids: Zondervan, 1965.

The Living Bible Paraphrased (Kenneth N. Taylor; evangelical best selling easy to read paraphrase; also marketed as The Book). Wheaton, IL: Tyndale House, 1971.

Old Testament Translation:

New Jewish Publication Society Bible (Jewish scholars; widely acclaimed new translation). Philadelphia: Jewish Publication Society, 1982.

New Testament Translations:

The New Testament in Modern English (J. B. Phillips; first rate translation/ paraphrase acclaimed and widely used by mainstream Christians, uses vivid colloquial language to make meaning clear). New York: Macmillan Company, 1958, revised, 1972.

The New Testament in Modern Speech (Richard Francis Weymouth and revised by J. A. Robertson; acclaimed for its fresh insight). New York: Harper and Row, 1929.

MULTIPLE TRANSLATIONS SIDE BY SIDE WITH THE KING JAMES

The Bible from 26 Translations (every line of the King James Version along with several variations selected from 26 translations; like having a library of more than 30 translations). Grand Rapids: Baker Book House, 1988.

The New Laymen's Parallel Bible (King James Version, New International Version, Living Bible, and Revised Standard Version side by side). Grand Rapids: Zondervan, 1981.

The Comparative Study Bible (King James Version, New International Version, New American Standard, and Amplified Bible side by side). Grand Rapids: Zondervan, 1984.

Eight Translation New Testament (King James Version, Revised Standard Version, New International Version, New English Bible, Jerusalem Bible, Phillips Modern English, and Living Bible side by side). Wheaton, IL: Tyndale House, 1974.

The New Testament in Four Versions (King James Version, Revised Standard Version, Phillips Modern English and the New English Bible side by side). Washington DC: Christianity Today, 1965.

BIBLE CONCORDANCES

Strong's Exhaustive Concordance of the Bible (includes every word in Bible text with a number keyed to a dictionary of Hebrew and Greek originals with English definitions). New York: Thomas Nelson, 1979.

Young's An Analytical Concordance to the Bible (includes every word in Bible text under Hebrew and Greek originals with literal meaning). New York: Thomas Nelson, 1982.

Cruden's Complete Concordance to the Bible (a concise concordance). Grand Rapids: Zondervan, 1949.

Phrase Concordance of the Bible (a concordance of phrases). New York: Thomas Nelson, 1986.

TOPICAL BIBLES/SUBJECT INDEXES

Nave's Topical Bible (Orville Nave). Byron Center, MI: Associated Publishers, 1970.

The Power of God to Heal (George F. Garland). Mamaroneck, NY: Guideform Press, 1973.

Subject Guide to Bible Stories (George F. Garland). Westport, CT: Greenwood Publishing Co., 1969.

BIBLE LEXICONS/WORD STUDIES

Theological Dictionary of the New Testament, abridged one volume (G. W. Bromley trans., G. Kittel and G. Fredrich). Grand Rapids: Eerdmans, 1985.

Theological Word Book of the Old Testament, 2 vols. (R. L. Harris, G. L. Archer, B. K. Waltke). Chicago: Moody Press, 1980.

Vine's Expository Dictionary of Biblical Words (W. E. Vine, Merrill F. Unger, William White, eds.) includes both Old and New Testaments. Nashville: Thomas Nelson, 1984.

The Hebrew-Greek Key Study Bible, KJV (Spiros Zodhiates). Grand Rapids: Baker Book House, 1984.

The Language of the King James Bible (Melvin E. Elliott). Garden City, NY: Doubleday, 1967.

Old Testament Light (George M. Lamsa). San Francisco: Harper and Row, 1964.

Gospel Light (George M. Lamsa). San Francisco: Harper and Row, 1939.

New Testament Commentary (George M. Lamsa). Philadelphia: A. J. Holman, 1945.

The Bible Word Book (R. Bridges and L. A. Weigle). New York: Thomas Nelson, 1960.

BIBLE DICTIONARIES

The New Westminster Dictionary of the Bible (Henry Snyder Gehman, ed.). Philadelphia: Westminster Press, 1970.

The Interpreter's Dictionary to the Bible, 5 vols. (George A. Buttrick and Keith R. Crim, eds.). Nashville: Abingdon Press, 1976.

Harper's Bible Dictionary (Paul J. Achtemeier, ed.). San Francisco: Harper & Row, 1985.

Nelson's Illustrated Bible Dictionary (Herbert Lockyear, ed.). Thomas Nelson, 1986.

New International Dictionary of the Bible (J. D. Douglas and Merrill C. Tenney, eds.). Grand Rapids: Zondervan, 1987.

The Dictionary of Bible and Religion (William H. Gentz, ed.). Nashville: Abingdon Press, 1986.

Young Peoples' Bible Dictionary (Barbara Smith). Philadelphia: Westminster, 1965.

Hastings' Dictionary of the Bible (James Hastings, Frederick C. Grant, H. H. Rowley, eds.). New York: Charles Scribner's Sons, 1963.

BIBLE ATLASES/HISTORIES/MAPS

Penguin Shorter Atlas of the Bible (L. H. Grollenberg). London: Penguin Books, 1978.

Reader's Digest Atlas of the Bible (J. L. Gardner). Pleasantville, NY: Reader's Digest, 1981.

Harper Atlas of the Bible (J. P. Prichard, ed.) New York: Harper and Row,1987.

Macmillan Bible Atlas (Y. Aharoni and M. Avi-Yonah). New York: Macmillan, 1977.

Macmillan Atlas History of Christianity (F. H. Little). New York: Macmillan, 1974.

The Golden Bible Atlas (Samuel Terrien). New York: Golden Press, 1957.

Westminster Historical Atlas to the Bible (G. E. Wright and F. Filson). Philadelphia: Westminster Press, 1956.

Rand McNally Bible Atlas (E. G. Kraeling). New York: Rand McNally, 1956.

Atlas of the Bible (L. H. Grollenberg). New York: Nelson, 1956.

Atlas of the Biblical World (D. Baly and A. Tushingham). New York: World, 1971.

Oxford Bible Atlas (H. G. May). New York: Oxford, 1974.

The Graphic Bible (Lewis Browne). New York: Macmillan, 1961.

Discovering the Biblical World (Harry Thomas Frank). Maplewood, NJ: Hammond, 1975.

Archaeology of the Bible: Book by Book (Goalyah Cornfeld and David Noel Freedman). San Francisco: Harper and Row, 1976.

BIBLE COMMENTARIES--ONE VOLUME

The Interpreter's One Volume Commentary on the Bible (Charles M. Laymon, ed.). Nashville: Abingdon Press, 1971.

Peake's Commentary on the Bible (Matthew Black and H. H. Rowley). Nashville: Thomas Nelson, 1962.

The Abingdon Bible Commentary (Frederick Eiselen, Edwin Lewis, David G. Downey, eds.). Nashville: Abingdon Press, 1929.

Dummelow's Commentary on the Holy Bible (J. R. Dummelow, ed.). New York: Macmillan, 1948.

The New Jerome Biblical Commentary (Raymond E. Brown, Joseph Fitzmyer, Roland E. Murphy, eds.). Englewood Cliffs: Prentice-Hall, 1990.

Commentary on the Whole Bible (Robert Jamieson, A. R. Fausset, David Brown, eds.). Grand Rapids: Zondervan, 1961.

The International Bible Commentary (F. F. Bruce). Grand Rapids: Zondervan, 1985.

The following commentaries are listed somewhat in the order of difficulty. Typically various volumes in each series are written by different scholars specializing in that book of the Bible.

The Interpreter's Bible (George A. Buttrick, Walter R. Bowier, Paul Scherer, John Knox, Samuel Terrien, eds.), 12 vols. Nashville: Abingdon, 1957.

The Expositor's Bible Commentary (Frank E. Gaebelein, general ed.), 12 volumes. Grand Rapids: Zondervan, 1976--.

Word Biblical Commentary (David A. Hubbard and Glenn W. Barker, general eds.), 52 volumes projected. Waco: Word Books, 1982--.

Barclay's Daily Study Bible (William Barclay), 18 volumes. Philadelphia: Westminster Press, 1975.

Westminster Daily Study Bible (Old Testament), 24 volumes. Philadelphia: Westminster Press, 1975.

The Cambridge Bible Commentary of the New English Bible (P. R. Ackroyd, A. R. C. Leaney, and J. W. Packer general eds.), 30 plus volumes. London: Cambridge University Press, 1966--.

Harper's New Testament Commentaries (Henry Chadwick, general ed.), 16 volumes. New York: Harper and Row, 1966.

The Old Testament Library (G. Ernest Wright, John Bright, James Barr, Peter Ackroyd, general eds.), 30 volumes. Philadelphia: Westminster, 1962--.

The Tyndale Old Testament Commentaries (D. J. Wiseman, general ed.), 18 volumes. Downers Grove: Inter-Varsity Press, 1964--.

The Tyndale New Testament Commentaries (R. V. G. Tasker, general ed.), 20 volumes. Grand Rapids: Eerdmans Publishing Co., 1957--.

New International Commentary on the Old Testament (R. K. Harrison, general ed.), 20 volumes. Grand Rapids: Eerdmans Publishing Co., 1976--.

New International Commentary on the New Testament (F. F. Bruce, general ed.), 18 volumes. Grand Rapids: Eerdmans Publishing Co., 1951--.

New Century Bible Commentary (Ronald E. Clements and Matthew Black, general eds.), 30 vols. Grand Rapids: Eerdmans Publishing Co., 1966--.

The Laymen's Bible Commentary (H. Balmer Kelly, ed.), 25 volumes. Atlanta: John Knox, 1960--.

The Bible Student's Commentary (Edward Viening, ed.) 62 volumes projected. Grand Rapids: Zondervan, 1981--.

The International Critical Commentary (S. R. Driver, A. Plummer, C. A. Briggs and others, eds.), 50 volumes. Edinburgh: T & T Clark, 1895--.

The Anchor Bible (W. G. Albright and David Noel Freedman, eds.), 40 volumes. Garden City: Doubleday, 1964--.

Hermeneia--A Critical and Historical Commentary (Frank Moore Cross, J. Helmut Koester and others, eds.), 16 volumes plus. Philadelphia: Fortress Press, 1971--.

New Testament Commentary (William Hendriksen and Simon J. Kistenmaker), 12 volumes. Grand Rapids: Baker Book House, 1953--.

Harper's Encyclopedia of Bible Life (M. S. and J. L. Miller). New York: Harper and Row, 1978.

Pictorial Biblical Encyclopedia. New York: Macmillan Co., 1964.

Everyday Life in Bible Times. Washington, DC: National Geographic Society, 1967.

Handbook of Life in Bible Times (J. A. Thompson). Downers Grove: Intervarsity Press, 1985.

Great People of the Bible and How They Lived. Pleasantville, NY: Reader's Digest Association, 1974.

Manners and Customs of Bible Lands (Fred H. Wight). Chicago: Moody Press, 1953.

Eerdman's Family Encyclopedia of the Bible (Pat Alexander, ed.). Grand Rapids: Eerdmans, 1978.

Bible Encyclopedia for Children (Cecil Northcott). Philadelphia: Westminster Press, 1964.

Life in Bible Times (Robert Henderson and Ian Gould). New York: Rand McNally, 1967.

Who's Who in the Bible (Joan Comay, Old Testament and Apocrypha, and Ronald Brownrigg, New Testament). New York: Bonanza Books, 1980.

People from the Bible (OT, Martin Woodrow; NT, E. P. Sanders). Wilton, CT: Morehouse-Barlow, 1987.

Animals, Birds and Plants of the Bible (William S. Smith). Nashville: Abingdon, 1971.

BIBLE STUDY HANDBOOKS/STUDY GUIDES

The Illustrated Bible Handbook (Edward P. Blair). Nashville: Abingdon, 1985.

The Bible Handbook (Thomas L. Leishman and Arthur T. Lewis). New York: Thomas Nelson, 1965.

Bible Study Source Book (Donald E. Demary). Grand Rapids: Zondervan, 1964.

Halley's Bible Handbook (H. H. Halley). Grand Rapids: Zondervan, 1959.

The Thompson Chain-Reference Bible Survey (Howard A. Hanke). Waco, TX: Word Books, 1981.

Getting Better Acquainted With Your Bible (Berenice Myers Shotwell). Kennebunkport, ME: Shadwold Press, 1972.

Studies in the Bible for the Modern Reader (Edyth Armstrong Hoyt). Ann Arbor: Edwards Brothers, 1952.

The Modern Reader's Bible (Richard C. Moulton). New York: Macmillan, 1926.

Syllabus for Adult and College Bible Students (Ann Putcamp). Elsah, IL: Principia College, 1966.

The Bible and the Historical Design (Mable A. Dominick). Norwood, MA: The Pilgrim Press, 1936.

APPENDIX II

FOR FURTHER READING

"You study the Scriptures because
you think that in them you will find
eternal life. And these very Scriptures speak about me!"
-Christ Jesus (John 5:39)
Today's English Version

The books listed on the following pages vary widely in scholarship and point of view. One author may contradict another, or, citing the same information, arrive at quite different conclusions. But each book in its own way may prove helpful for further Biblical insight and understanding. Of course, only a sampling of the thousands of such books available are included here. A few books listed are now out of print, but have been included because of their influence on my own study.

UNDERSTANDING AND APPRECIATING THE BIBLE

Anderson, Bernhard W., Rediscovering the Bible. N.Y.: Association Press, 1951
Chase, Mary Ellen, The Bible and the Common Reader. N.Y.: Macmillan, 1944.
Chute, Marchette, The Search for God. New York: E. P. Dutton, 1941.
Dodd, C. H., The Bible Today. Cambridge: Cambridge University Press, 1965.
Eddy, Mary Baker, Science and Health with Key to the Scriptures. Boston: The First Church of Christ, Scientist, 1909, 1971.
Goodspeed, Edgar J., How to Read the Bible. Philadelphia: John C. Winston Co., 1946.
Greenwood, Samuel, Footsteps of Israel. Privately published, 1930.
Moyle, Frank W., About the Bible. New York: Charles Scribner's Sons, 1956.
Neil, William, Modern Man Looks at the Bible. New York: Association Press, 1958.

BIBLE BACKGROUND AND HISTORY

Avi-Yonah, Michael and E. Kraeling, Our Living Bible. New York: McGraw-Hill, 1962.
Breasted, James Henry, Ancient Times, A History of the Early World. New York: Ginn and Company, reprinted, 1967.
Berrett, Lamar C., Discovering the World of the Bible. Nashville: Thomas Nelson, 1979.
Deen, Edith, All the Women of the Bible. New York: Harper, 1955.
Finegan, Jack, Light from the Ancient Past: The Archeological Background of the Hebrew-Christian Religion, 2 vols. Princeton: Princeton University Press, 1959.
Finegan, Jack, The Archeology of the New Testament. Princeton: Princeton University Press, 1969.
Keller, Werner (trans. by William Neil), The Bible as History, a Confirmation of the Book of Books. New York: William Morrow and Company, 1956.
Kenyon, K. M., The Bible and Recent Archaeology. Atlanta: John Knox Press, 1978.
Leishman, Thomas Linton, The Continuity of the Bible, 5 vols. Boston: Christian Science Publishing Society, 1966-77.
Leishman, Thomas Linton, The Interrelation of Old and New Testaments. New York: Vantage Press, 1968.

Swidler, Leonard, <u>Biblical Affirmations of Women</u>. Philadelphia: Westminster Press, 1979.

Wright, G. Ernest, <u>Biblical Archaeology</u>. Philadelphia: Westminster Press, 1962.

HOW THE BIBLE CAME TO BE

Bruce, F. F., <u>History of the Bible in English</u>. Fairlawn, NJ: Oxford University Press, 1978.

Ewert, David, <u>From Ancient Tablets to Modern Translation</u>. Grand Rapids: Zondervan, 1983.

Gilmore, Albert F., <u>The Bible: Beacon Light of History</u>. Boston: Associated Authors, 1935.

Leishman, Thomas Linton, <u>Our Ageless Bible, from Early Manuscripts to Modern Versions</u>. New York: Nelson and Sons, 1960.

Opfell, Olga S., <u>The King James Bible Translators</u>. Jefferson, NC: McFarland and Co., 1982.

Metzger, Bruce, <u>The Text of the New Testament</u>. Fairlawn, NJ: Oxford University Press, 1968.

Paine, Gustavus S., <u>The Learned Men</u> (on the translators of the King James Version). New York: Thomas Y. Crowell Company, 1959.

ON THE OLD TESTAMENT

Albright, William F., <u>Biblical Period from Abraham to Ezra</u>. New York: Harper Torchbooks, 1963.

Anderson, Bernhard W., <u>The Living World of the Old Testament</u>. Englewood Cliffs: Prentice-Hall, 1975.

Anderson, Bernhard W., <u>Understanding the Old Testament</u>, Fourth Edition. New York: Prentice-Hall, 1986.

Bright, John, <u>A History of Israel</u>. Philadelphia: Westminster Press, 1981.

Bruce, F. F., <u>Israel and the Nations</u>. Grand Rapids: Eerdmans, 1963.

Chase, Mary Ellen, <u>Life and Language of the Old Testament</u>. New York: W. W. Norton Co., 1955.

Davidson, R., <u>The Old Testament</u>. Philadelphia: Lippincott, 1964.

De Vaux, Roland, <u>Ancient Israel</u>. New York: McGraw-Hill, 1961.

Drane, John, <u>Old Testament Faith</u>. San Francisco: Harper and Row, 1986.

Drane, John, <u>The Old Testament Story</u>. San Francisco: Harper and Row, 1983.

Hayes, J. H., <u>An Introduction to Old Testament Study</u>. Nashville: Abingdon Press, 1979.

Lace, O. Jessie, <u>Understanding the Old Testament</u>. Cambridge: University Press, 1972.

Neil, William, <u>Can We Trust the Old Testament?</u> NY: Seabury Press, 1979.

Rad, Gerhard von, <u>Old Testament Theology</u>, 2 vols. New York: Harper and Row, 1962.

Rowley, H. H., <u>The Faith of Israel</u>. Philadelphia: Westminster Press, 1983.

Vawter, Bruce, <u>On Genesis</u>. Garden City: Doubleday, 1977.

ON THE PROPHETS

Anderson, B. W., The Eighth Century Prophets. Philadelphia: Fortress Press, 1978.

Carroll, R. P., Jeremiah. Philadelphia: Westminster Press, 1986.

Chase, Mary Ellen, The Prophets for the Common Reader. New York: W. W. Norton and Co., 1963.

Gottwald, Norman K., All the Kingdoms of the Earth. New York: Harper and Row, 1964.

Heaton, E. W., The Old Testament Prophets. New York: Penguin Books, 1958.

Holladay, W. L., Jeremiah: Spokesman Out of Time. NY: Pilgrim Press, 1974.

Koch, Klaus, The Prophets, Vols. I and II, Philadelphia: Fortress Press 1982.

Kraeling, Emil G., Commentary on the Prophets, volumes I, II. Nashville: Thomas Nelson, 1966.

Mowvley, H., Reading the Old Testament Prophets Today. Atlanta: John Knox Press, 1979.

Phillips, J. B., Four Prophets: Amos, Hosea, First Isaiah, Micah (a translation). New York: Macmillan Co., 1963.

Rad, Gerhard von, The Message of the Prophets. New York: Harper and Row, 1968.

Smith, J. M. Powis, The Prophets and Their Times, 2nd ed., rev. by William A. Irwin. Chicago: University of Chicago Press, 1941.

Williams, W., The Prophets, Pioneers to Christianity. New York: Abingdon, 1956.

ON THE PSALMS

Anderson, Bernhard W., Out of the Depths: Psalms Speak Today. Philadelphia: Westminster Press, 1983.

Chase, Mary Ellen, Psalms for the Common Reader. New York: W. W. Norton, 1962.

Gunkel, H., The Psalms. Philadelphia: Fortress, 1967.

Hayes, J. H., Understanding the Psalms. Valley Forge, PA: Judson Press, 1976.

Hoyt, Edyth Armstrong, Studies in the Psalms. Chicago: Associated Authors, 1937.

Knight, William Allen, The Song of Our Syrian Guest (on the 23rd Psalm). Boston, The Pilgrim Press, n.d.

Phillips, John, Exploring the Psalms. Neptune, NJ: Loizeaux Bros., 1988.

Terrien, Samuel, The Psalms and Their Meaning for Today. Indianapolis: Bobbs-Merrill Co., 1950.

Westermann, Claus, The Living Psalms. Grand Rapids: Eerdmans, 1989.

BETWEEN THE TESTAMENTS

Cross, Frank Moore Jr., The Ancient Library of Qumran and Modern Biblical Studies. Grand Rapids: Baker Book House, 1961.

Gowan, D. E., <u>Bridge Between the Testaments</u>. Pickwick Press, 1976.

LaSor, W. S., <u>The Dead Sea Scrolls and the New Testament</u>. Grand Rapids: Eerdmans, 1972.

Neusner, J., <u>Judaism in the Beginning of Christianity</u>. Philadelphia: Fortress Press, 1984.

Pfeiffer, Robert H., <u>History of New Testament Times with an Introduction to the Apocrypha</u>. New York: Harper and Brothers, 1949.

Metzger, Bruce M., <u>An Introduction to the Apocrypha</u>. New York: Oxford University Press, 1957.

Trevor, John C., <u>The Untold Story of Qumran</u>. Westwood, NJ: Fleming H. Revell Co., 1960.

ON THE NEW TESTAMENT

Barrett, C. K., <u>The New Testament Background: Selected Documents</u>. New York: Harper and Row, 1961.

Drane, John, <u>Introducing the New Testament</u>. San Francisco: Harper and Row, 1986.

Filson, Floyd V., <u>A New Testament History, The Story of the Emerging Church</u>. Philadelphia: Westminster Press, 1964.

Grant, Robert M., <u>Formation of the New Testament</u>. New York: Harper and Row, 1965.

Kee, Howard Clark and others, <u>Understanding the New Testament</u>. Englewood Cliffs, NJ: Prentice-Hall, 1973.

Kummel, W. G., <u>Introduction to the New Testament</u>. Nashville: Abingdon, 1974

Loshe, E., <u>The Formation of the New Testament</u>. Nashville: Abingdon, 1981.

Metzger, Bruce, <u>The New Testament: Its Background, Growth and Content</u>, 2nd ed. Nashville: Abingdon Press, 1983.

Neill, Stephen, <u>Jesus Through Many Eyes: Introduction to the Theology of the New Testament</u>. Philadelphia: Fortress Press, 1976.

Reicke, Bo, <u>The New Testament Era: The World of the Bible from 500 B. C. to A. D. 100</u>, (trans. by David E. Green). Philadelphia: Westminster, 1968.

Robinson, John A. T., <u>Redating the New Testament</u>. Philadelphia: Westminster, 1976.

Rowlingson, Donald T., <u>Introduction to New Testament Study</u>. New York: Macmillan, 1956.

ON NON-CANONICAL CHRISTIAN WRITINGS

Cameron, Ron (ed.) <u>The Other Gospels: Non-Canonical Gospel Texts</u>. Philadelphia: Westminster Press, 1982.

<u>Early Christian Writings: The Apostolic Fathers</u> (trans. by Maxwell Staniforth). New York: Dorset Press, 1968.

Goodspeed, Edgar J. and Robert M. Grant, <u>A History of Early Christian Literature</u> (revised and enlarged). Chicago: The University Press, 1966.

Pagels, Elaine, <u>The Gnostic Gospels</u>. New York: Random House, 1979.

Robinson, James M. (ed.), <u>The Nag Hammadi Library</u> (Gnostic writings). New York: Harper and Row, 1977.

ON CHRIST JESUS

Barclay, William, <u>Jesus of Nazareth</u>. London: Collins-World, 1977.

Bauman, Edward W., <u>The Life and Teachings of Jesus</u>. Philadelphia: Westminster Press, 1960.

Beasley, Norman, <u>This is the Promise</u>. NY: Duell, Sloan and Pearce, 1957.

Cassels, Louis, <u>The Real Jesus: How He Lived and What He Taught</u>. Garden City, NY: Doubleday, 1968.

Chute, Marchette, <u>Jesus of Israel</u>. New York: E. P. Dutton and Co., 1961.

Dakes, John A., <u>Christ Jesus</u> (translation of the four Gospels with notes). Chicago: Avalon Publishing Co., 1940.

Danker, Frederick, <u>Jesus and the New Age</u>. St. Louis: Clayton, 1972

Dodd, C. H., <u>The Founder of Christianity</u>. New York: Macmillan, 1970.

Dunn, James D. G., <u>The Evidence for Jesus</u>. Philadelphia: Westminster Press, 1985.

Gilmore, Albert F., <u>Who Was This Nazarene? A Challenging and Definitive Biography of the Master</u>. New York: Prentice-Hall, 1945.

Grant, Michael, <u>Jesus: An Historian's Review of the Gospels</u>. New York: Charles Scribner's Sons, 1977.

Habermas, Gary R., <u>Ancient Evidence for the Life of Jesus</u>. Nashville: Thomas Nelson, 1984.

Kee, Howard Clark, <u>Jesus in History, An Approach to the Study of the Gospels</u>. New York: Harcourt, Brace, Jovanovich, 1977.

Klausner, Joseph, <u>Jesus of Nazareth</u>. Boston: Beacon, 1961.

Morton, H. V., <u>In the Steps of Jesus</u>. New York: Dodd, Mead, 1958.

Neil, William, <u>The Life and Teachings of Jesus</u>. Philadelphia: Lippincott, 1965.

Olmstead, Albert T. E., <u>Jesus, in the Light of History</u>. NY: Scribner's, 1942.

Perrin, Norman, <u>Jesus and Language of the Kingdom</u>. Philadelphia: Fortress Press, 1980.

Ward, Kaari (ed.) <u>Jesus and His Times</u>. Pleasantville, NY: Reader's Digest Association, 1987.

ON THE DISCIPLES

Barclay, William, <u>The Master's Men</u>, Nashville: Abingdon, 1959.

Barker, William P., <u>Twelve Who Were Chosen</u>. Westwood, NJ: Fleming H. Revell Co., 1957.

Bruce, F. F., <u>Peter, Stephen, James and John, Studies in Non-Pauline Christianity</u>. Grand Rapids: William B. Eerdmans Publishing Co., 1979.

Goodspeed, Edgar J., <u>The Twelve: The Story of Christ's Apostles</u>. New York: Henry Holt and Co., 1957.

Smith, Asbury, <u>The Twelve Christ Chose</u>. New York: Harper and Row, 1958.

ON THE TEACHINGS OF JESUS

Barclay, William, <u>The Mind of Jesus</u>. New York: Harper and Row, 1961.

Davies, W. D., <u>The Setting of the Sermon on the Mount</u>. Cambridge: University Press, 1964.

Dodd, C. H., <u>The Parables of the Kingdom</u>. New York: Harper and Row, 1981.

Hendrickx, H., <u>The Sermon on the Mount</u>. Philadelphia: Winston, 1984.

Jeremias, Joachim, <u>The Parables of Jesus</u>. New York: Charles Scribners, 1972.

Kistemaker, Simon J., <u>The Parables of Jesus</u>. Grand Rapids: Baker House, 1980.

Neil, William, <u>The Difficult Sayings of Jesus</u>. Grand Rapids: Eerdmans, 1975.

Robinson, John A. T., <u>Jesus and His Coming</u>. Philadelphia: Westminster, 1979.

Seagren, Daniel R., <u>The Parables</u>. Wheaton: Tyndale, 1978.

Stein, R. H., <u>An Introduction to the Parables of Jesus</u>. Philadelphia: Westminster, 1981.

Stein, R. H., <u>The Method and Message of Jesus' Teachings</u>. Philadelphia, Westminster, 1978.

Trench, R. C., <u>Notes on the Parables of Our Lord</u>. Grand Rapids: Baker, 1948.

Trench, R. C., <u>Notes on the Miracles of Our Lord</u>. Grand Rapids: Baker, 1949.

Trueblood, Elton, <u>The Humor of Christ</u>. New York: Harper and Row, 1964.

ON PAUL

Barclay, William, <u>The Mind of Paul</u>. New York: Harper and Row, 1958.

Bornkamm, G., <u>Paul</u> (trans. by D. M. G. Stalker). New York: Harper and Row, 1971.

Buckmaster, Henrietta, <u>Paul, A Man Who Changed the World</u>. New York: McGraw-Hill Book Co., 1965.

Conybeare, W. J., and J. S. Howson, <u>The Life and Epistles of St. Paul</u>. Grand Rapids: Eerdmans, 1959.

Davies, W. D., <u>Paul and Rabbinic Judaism</u>. New York: Harper and Row, 1970.

Dodd, C. H., <u>The Meaning of Paul for Today</u>. New York: Meridian Books, 1937.

Drane, John, <u>Paul</u>. New York: Harper and Row, 1976.

Drummond, Henry, <u>The Greatest Thing in the World</u> (on I Corinthians 13). Westwood, NJ: Fleming H. Revell Co.

Ellis, E. E., <u>Paul's Use of the Old Testament</u>. Grand Rapids: Baker, 1981.

Goodspeed, Edgar J., <u>Paul</u>. Philadelphia: John C. Winston Co., 1947.

Lyall, Francis, <u>Slaves, Citizens, Sons: Legal Metaphors in the Epistles</u>. Grand Rapids: Zondervan, 1984.

Morton, H. V., <u>In the Steps of St. Paul</u>. New York: Dodd, Mead, 1958.

Sanders, E. P., <u>Paul, the Law and the Jewish People</u>. Philadelphia: Fortress Press, 1983.

Selby, Donald J., <u>Toward the Understanding of Paul</u>. New York: Prentice-Hall, 1962.

ON THE APOCALYPSE OF JOHN

Caird, G. B., A Commentary on the Revelation of St. John the Divine. New York: Harper and Row, 1966.

Carrington, Philip, The Meaning of the Revelation. New York: Macmillan, 1931.

Charles, R. H., A Critical and Exegetical Commentary on the Revelation of St. John, 2 vols. Edinburgh: T & T Clark, 1920.

Chute, Marchette, The End of the Search (also commentary on Acts and Letters). New York: North River Press, 1947.

Hoyt, Edyth Armstrong, Studies in the Apocalypse of John of Patmos. Ann Arbor: Edwards Brothers, 1952.

Kiddle, Martin, The Revelation of St. John. New York: Harper, 1940.

Lilje, Hanns, The Last Book of the Bible (trans. by Olive Wyon). Philadelphia: Fortress Press, 1957.

Minear, Paul S., I Saw a New Earth: An Introduction to the Visions of the Apocalypse. Cleveland: Corpus Books, 1968.

Scott, Ernest F., The Book of Revelation. New York: Scribners, 1940.

Swete, Henry Barclay, The Apocalypse of St. John. New York: Macmillan, 1906.

Tomlinson, Irving C., The Revelation of St. John, An Open Book. Privately published, 1922.

ON EARLY CHRISTIANITY

Bettenson, Henry (ed.) Documents of the Christian Church. London: Oxford University Press, 1963.

Bultman, Rudolf, Primitive Christianity. Cleveland: World, 1956.

Eusebius, The History of the Church from Christ to Constantine (trans. by G. A. Williamson). New York: Dorset Press, 1965.

Frend, W. H. C., The Early Church. Philadelphia: Fortress Press, 1982.

Frend, W. H. C., The Rise of Christianity. Philadelphia: Fortress Press, 1984.

Fridrichsen, Anton, The Problem of Miracle in Primitive Christianity. Minneapolis: Augsburg, 1972.

Harnack, Adolf, The Mission and Expansion of Christianity in the First Three Centuries (trans. by James Moffatt). NY: Harper and Brothers, 1961.

Hengel, Martin, Acts and the History of Earliest Christianity. Philadelphia: Fortress Press, 1979.

Lietzmann, Hans, A History of the Early Church (trans. by Bertram Lee Woolf). New York: Meridian Books, World Publishing Co., 1961.

Lohse, E., The First Christians. Philadelphia: Fortress, 1983.

Nock, Arthur Darby, Early Gentile Christianity and Its Hellenistic Background. New York: Harper Torchbook, 1964.

MacMullen, Ramsay, Christianizing the Roman Empire: A.D.10-400. New Haven: Yale University Press, 1984.

Malherbe, A. J., Social Aspects of Early Christianity. Philadelphia: Fortress Press, 1983.

134

Marty, Martin, <u>A Short History of Christianity</u>, revised and expanded. Philadelphia: Fortress Press, 1986.

Meeks, Wayne A., <u>The First Urban Christians</u>. New Haven: Yale University Press, 1983.

Phillips, J. B., <u>New Testament Christianity</u>. New York: Macmillan Co., 1956.

Phillips, J. B., <u>Ring of Truth</u>. New York: Macmillan Co., 1967.

Weiss, Johannes, <u>Earliest Christianity, A History of the Period A. D. 30--150</u> (2 vols.). New York: Harper Torchbooks, 1959.

ON CHRISTIAN HEALING

<u>A Century of Christian Science Healing.</u> Boston: The Christian Science Publishing Society, 1966.

Darling, Frank, <u>Biblical Healing: Hebrew and Christian Roots</u>. Boulder, CO: Vista Publications, 1989.

Darling, Frank, <u>Christian Healing in the Middle Ages and Beyond</u>. Boulder, CO: Vista Publications, 1990.

Drury, Michael, <u>Every Whit Whole: The Adventure of Spiritual Healing</u>. New York: Walker and Co., 1978.

Eddy, Mary Baker, <u>Science and Health with Key to the Scriptures</u>. Boston: The First Church of Christ, Scientist, 1909, 1971.

Frost, Evelyn, <u>Christian Healing</u>. London: A. R. Bowbray & Co., 1954.

Harrell, David Edwin Jr., <u>All Things Are Possible: The Healing and Charismatic Revivals in Modern America</u>. Indiana University Press, 1975.

Ikin, A. Graham, <u>New Concepts of Healing</u>. New York: Association Press, 1956.

Kelsey, Morton, <u>Psychology, Medicine and Christian Healing, A Revised and Expanded Edition of Healing & Christianity</u>. San Francisco: Harper and Row, 1975.

Lawrence, R. <u>Christian Healing Rediscovered</u>. Downers Grove:InterVarsity,1980

Oursler, Will, <u>The Healing Power of Faith</u>. New York: Hawthorne Books, 1957.

Peel, Robert, <u>Health and Medicine in the Christian Science Tradition</u>. New York: Crossroad, 1988.

Peel, Robert, <u>Spiritual Healing in a Scientific Age</u>. San Francisco: Harper and Row, 1987.

Sanford, John A., <u>Healing and Wholeness</u>. New York: Paulist Press, 1977.

Wimber, John, <u>Power Healing</u>. San Francisco: Harper and Row, 1987.

ON LATER CHRISTIAN DEVELOPMENTS

Bach, Marcus, <u>They Have Found a Faith</u>. New York: Bobbs-Merrill, 1946.

Bainton, Roland H., <u>The Reformation of the Sixteenth Century</u>. Boston: Beacon Press, 1952.

Barraclough, Geoffrey (ed.), <u>The Christian World: A Social and Cultural History</u>. New York: Harry N. Abrams, Inc., 1981.

Brantl, George (ed.), <u>Catholicism</u>. New York: George Braziller, 1962.

Brown, D. Mackenzie, <u>Ultimate Concern: Tillich in Dialogue</u>. New York: Harper and Row, 1965.

Dustin, J. Leslie (ed.), <u>Protestantism</u>. New York: George Braziller, 1962.

Ferm, Vergillius (ed.), <u>Religion in the Twentieth Century</u>. New York: The Philosophical Library, 1948.

Frerichs, Ernest (ed.), <u>The Bible and Bibles in America</u>. Atlanta: Scholars Press, 1988.

Gilmore, Albert F., <u>Links in Christianity's Chain</u>. Boston: The Waters Co., 1938.

Gottschalk, Stephen, <u>The Emergence of Christian Science in American Religious Life</u>. Berkeley: University of California Press, 1973.

Harnack, Adolf, <u>What is Christianity?</u> New York: Harper Torchbooks, 1957.

James, E. O., <u>Christianity and Other Religions</u>. Philadelphia: Lippincott,1968.

Johnson, Paul, <u>A History of Christianity</u>. New York: Atheneum, 1976.

Kittler, Glenn D., <u>Profiles of Faith</u>. New York: Coward-McCann, 1962.

Marty, Martin, <u>Our Faith</u>. New York: Pillar Books, 1976.

Micks, Marianne, <u>Introduction to Theology</u>. New York: Seabury Press, 1964.

Peel, Robert, <u>Christian Science, Its Encounter with American Culture</u>. New York: Henry Holt and Co., 1958.

Peel, Robert, <u>Mary Baker Eddy</u> (3 vols.) <u>The Years of Discovery</u>, <u>The Years of Trial</u>, <u>The Years of Authority</u>. New York: Henry Holt and Co., 1966, 1971, 1973.

Phillips, J. B., <u>Your God is Too Small</u>. New York: Macmillan, 1961.

Ramm, Bernard, <u>After Fundamentalism: The Future of Evangelical Theology</u>. NY: Harper and Row, 1983.

Robinson, John A. T., <u>Honest to God</u>. Philadelphia: Westminster, 1963.

Robinson, John A. T., <u>The New Reformation</u>. Philadelphia: Westminster, 1965.

Rosten, Leo, <u>A Guide to the Religions of America</u>. New York: Simon and Schuster, 1955.

Spence, Hartzell, <u>The Story of America's Religions</u>. New York: Holt, Rinehart and Winston, 1960.

<u>The Westminster Dictionary of Christian Theology</u> (Allen Richardson and John Bowden eds.). Philadelphia: Westminster Press, 1983.

ON RELIGIONS OF THE WORLD (including Christianity)

Bradley, David G., <u>A Guide to the World's Religions</u>. Englewood Cliffs, NJ: Prentice-Hall, 1963.

Browne, Lewis, <u>This Believing World</u>. New York: Macmillan Co., 1961.

Cranston, Ruth, <u>World Faith, the Story of the Religions of the United Nations</u>. New York: Harper and Brothers, 1949.

Editors of Life, <u>The World's Great Religions</u>. New York: Time, Inc., 1961.

Gaer, Joseph, <u>How the Great Religions Began</u>. New York: Dodd, Mead, 1954.

Hume, Robert E., <u>The World's Living Religions</u>. New York: Scribners, 1959.

Potter, Charles Francis, <u>The Faiths Men Live By</u>. Englewood Cliffs, NY: Prentice-Hall, 1954.

Schoeps, Hans-Joachim, <u>The Religions of Mankind</u> (trans. by Richard and Clara Winston). New York: Anchor Books, 1966.

Smith, Huston, <u>The Religions of Man</u>. New York: Harper Colophon, 1958.

APPENDIX III

FOR TEACHERS

Teaching
Learning
Lesson Planning
Teaching Methods
Worksheets

"Every inspired scripture has its use for teaching the truth and refuting error, or for reformation of manners and discipline in right living, so that the man who belongs to God may be efficient and equipped for good work of every kind."

II Timothy 3:16-17
New English Bible

There are few, if any, rewards for the Christian equal to that of opening the Book of Books to young people enrolled in a Sunday School. To the teacher goes the challenge to so teach the Scriptures that pupils will become life-long students of the Bible, that Paul's words to Timothy will apply to each pupil:

"Continue thou in the things which thou hast learned and hast been assured of, knowing of whom thou hast learned them; And that from a child thou hast known the holy scriptures, which are able to make thee wise unto salvation through faith which is in Christ Jesus. All scripture is given by inspiration of God, and is profitable for doctrine, for reproof, for correction, for instruction in righteousness, That the man of God may be perfect, throughly furnished unto all good works."

The successful Sunday School teacher is one who studies and plans, one who prepares for the class, one who combines inspiration with careful preparation. This requires great love for young people and personal dedication to a high goal. It requires an inquiring attitude and commitment to continued learning and study. Only the teacher who is a student can communicate to pupils the excitement of the discovery of learning. For learners must discover the truth of the Bible for themselves before they can make it their own.

The teacher provides the opportunities for learning, the environment in which learning can take place, but it is the learner who learns. In this climate setting there is no substitute for careful preparation. Teaching is not random. It is not incidental. It is not a smattering of this and that. Effective teaching is planned. The teacher has goals of what is expected to be accomplished in the next month, the next quarter, the next year.

But even more, the teacher turns to the Source of inspiration in seeking to communicate. The example of Christ Jesus is a model for the classroom. Jesus used a variety of methods as he taught his disciples, his students. He asked questions. He answered questions asked him. He used parables to illustrate a point he was making. He quoted from and referred to the Scriptures. He challenged thought. He encouraged self-examination. He used humor. And he lived the Truth he taught. No wonder he was called "Master"--teacher.

The following pages of general helps for teachers are designed to be useful in understanding something of the teaching/learning process and how to plan and conduct classes.

ABOUT TEACHING/LEARNING
POINTS TO CONSIDER

1. **Learning starts with what the learner knows,** not with what the teacher knows. Learners want to see benefits to themselves from the course. They require subject matter that is relevant to their objectives.

2. **The clearer, the more realistic and relevant the statement of desired outcomes (objectives), the better the learning.** If one can't see the target clearly, the chance of hitting it is not good. Be sure the learner knows what is expected.

3. **Learning needs to be applied immediately.** We learn what we use and practice. But mere practice does not make perfect; one can practice wrongly.

4. **Learning is increased by knowledge of results.** Appropriate responses should be acknowledged. Delayed approval or disapproval is not highly motivating. Learners need to be able to see and feel progress. Nothing motivates like success. We learn when we are rewarded and fail to learn when we feel "punished".

5. **We learn best what is meaningful to us.** The most meaningful learning experiences are those seen as a means to the learner's own goals. Learners want specific examples of practical and life-like situations related to their own needs and interests.

6. **We learn best when a variety of methods are used.** The worst teaching method is the one used all the time.

7. **Learning is more rapid and more likely to be retained when the learner is a participant rather than a listener.** Learners add enrichment to the class by calling on their own experiences and sharing their ideas.

8. **Learning by inquiry and discovery, rather than rote memorization, gives the learner practice in building insight.** By generalizing experiences, developing concepts, searching for meaning and an emerging principle, learners develop the habit of seeking relationships and unity in apparent diversity.

9. Dewey says, "**An ounce of experience is better than a ton of theory,** simply because it is only as an experience that any theory has vital and verifiable significance . . . . A theory apart from an experience cannot be definitely grasped even as theory."

10. **A learner wants to be treated as a person, not as a student.** Learners differ from fellow students and need personal attention and consideration of their interests, needs and concerns.

11. **A satisfied student will not only come back, but bring a friend.** A dissatisfied

student will quit the class either by dropping out or by pulling down a mental curtain and attending "in mental absentia".

12. **Learning must be organized for sequence.** The learner must perceive some organization in the material. Logical subject-matter is easier to learn, remember, and use, but this logic must make sense to the learner. It is the learner who will systematize, remember and use what is learned. A few points well learned are better than many points "covered" but not learned.

13. **The class atmosphere should be kept permissive and open.** The teacher should encourage those who express differing ideas and be sure that no one is embarrassed or put down.

14. **The teacher doesn't dominate conversation but rather encourages participation** and clear thinking and summarizes progress and brings the discussion to a logical conclusion.

15. **Discussion involves more than just having class members talk** or answer questions. Discussion involves working together to find the answer to an issue which is recognized as a need by students. Discussion is a cooperative search for truth. Students exchange opinions, secure information, clarify ideas, form attitudes, consider alternatives, seek new insights, and learn to appreciate and understand other points of view.

16. **When some students remain silent** it may be because they
    - agree with others so feel no need to speak
    - are slower to speak and someone always talks first
    - lack confidence in their ability to express themselves
    - feel they don't know the subject well enough
    - feel talking may be dangerous or that they may be rejected
    - have lost track of the discussion
    - fear to differ from the teacher

17. **When some students talk too much** it may be because they
    - want others to recognize their wisdom and knowledge
    - feel strongly about the subject or are over-enthusiastic
    - want to dominate the situation
    - want attention and enjoy an audience

18. **Learn to listen to students:**
    - Listen to understand what is meant, not to think of your reply.
    - Don't interpret too quickly what the pupil is trying to say.
    - Put yourself in the pupil's shoes; how does the world look to the pupil?
    - Put aside your own views and opinions for the moment.
    - We think faster than another speaks; keep thought on what the pupil is saying.

     -   Expect pupils to say what they mean in different words than you would use.

     -   Before you answer, sum up what you understand the pupil to be saying.

19. **When discipline problems occur think of discipline as growing in discipleship.** "Discipline" is from Latin word meaning "to learn".
    - Expect results from prayerful work and preparation.
    - Rejoice in every evidence of progress.
    - Look behind the problem behavior to its cause: a pupil's need for love, a pupil's need for self-discipline, a pupil's need for firmness, a pupil's lack of interest, whatever.

20. **Help pupils feel responsibility for their class.** We are all learners and teachers together. The class is not "your" class for them but _their_ class and you are the helper, facilitator.

21. **Qualifications for teaching:**
    - Love of children and young people so you can create a climate of mutual trust and respect.
    - Commitment to continuing your own learning.
    - Willingness to give time in planning, preparation and prayer.
    - Dedication to living Scripture--being an example.
    - Willingness to develop and improve educational skills.

22. **Two basic teaching styles:**
    1) <u>Content-centered teaching</u>
       Teacher concerned with subject matter, getting tasks done; relationship to pupils distant, cool, impersonal, formal; materials a major focus of program, used to present facts and information; teaching methods formal, impersonal, highly structured.
    2) <u>People-centered teaching</u>
       Teacher primarily concerned in stimulating discussion and seeing others grow; teacher flexible, open; relationship to pupils close, warm, personal, informal; materials incidental to program, used primarily to present problems and issues; teaching methods flexible, informal.

23. **Three kinds of learning:**
    1) <u>Skill learning</u>--psychomotor learning--learning to do
    2) <u>Knowledge learning</u>--cognitive learning--learning to think and understand
    3) <u>Attitude learning</u>--affective learning--learning to feel (love)

24. **How styles of teaching relate to kinds of learning:**

Highly Content Centered Teaching	**Mixed Content/People Centered Teaching**	**Highly People Centered Teaching**
▲	▲	▲
Skill Learning	**Knowledge Learning**	**Attitude Learning**

THE COURSE OUTLINE

A course outline can be likened to a road map: It shows the point from which we start, enables us to keep our objective in mind as we travel, and leads us to our goal by the most logical route.

These are the important steps in drawing the map for your course:

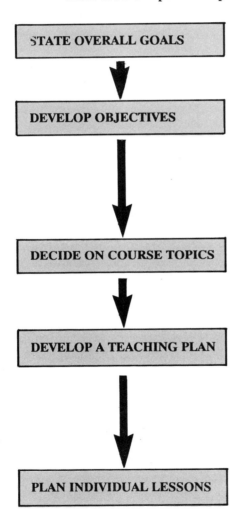

STATE OVERALL GOALS

List four to six over-all aims or goals you wish your students to achieve while you are their teacher.

DEVELOP OBJECTIVES

List your specific objectives in keeping with your goals. What do you want your students to <u>know</u>, what should they be able to <u>do</u>, how do you want them to <u>feel</u>? This will organize your thinking so that the rest of the work will fall into place.

DECIDE ON COURSE TOPICS

List the topical headings, and organize your material into the number of class sessions available to you.

DEVELOP A TEACHING PLAN

Keep your statement of objectives clearly in mind in terms of <u>knowledge</u>, <u>skills</u>, and <u>attitudes</u> to be acquired by the student, as you plan your course content and how you will teach it to your particular students.

PLAN INDIVIDUAL LESSONS

Plan individual lessons, activities, and home assignments on the basis of your overall plan. Be at least a month ahead of your class in detailed planning. Build in opportunity for flexibility.

TEACHER PRACTICE WORKSHEET I

Goals and Objectives

State one **Over-all Goal**:

_____
_____
_____
_____

Write three general objectives related to the goal which you would hope to accomplish over a 13-week period:
General Objectives for Quarter: (to accomplish in 13 weeks)

1. _____
_____

2. _____
_____

3. _____
_____
_____

Now take **one** of these objectives for the quarter and make it into three more specific **Objectives for a Month**: (to accomplish in 4 weeks)

1. _____
_____

2. _____
_____

3. _____
_____
_____

Now take **one** of these objectives for a month and make it into three more specific **Objectives for a Sunday**: (to accomplish in a single class session)

1. _____
_____

2. _____
_____

3. _____
_____

TEACHER PRACTICE WORKSHEET II

Teaching Plan for Quarter (Course Outline)

Over-all Goals: _____

Objectives for Quarter: _____

Course Topics: _____

Sundays	Objective	Bible Concept	Class Activity	Home Assignment
1st				
2nd				
3rd				
4th				
5th				
6th				
7th				
8th				
9th				
10th				
11th				
12th				
13th				

THE LESSON

As the **course outline** may be likened to a map, so the **lesson** may be likened to a particular stop-over on the way to the destination. Regardless of how long one has served, no teacher should enter the classroom without a lesson plan developed for that specific class. A vague aim will usually result in vague teaching. Do not necessarily adopt the lesson aim as stated in your Sunday School curriculum. That is an aim general enough for thousands of classes. Revise it to suit the needs of your class. Read the Scripture passage several times. Listen to what God communicates to you through it. Read the Scripture again along with the curriculum and related study materials. Keep in mind student needs. Then determine what you want the class to learn.

ASK YOURSELF BEFORE MAKING THE LESSON PLAN

1. Have the learners the necessary experience to understand the lesson?
2. How large an amount can they comprehend at one time?
3. What must I know to teach this lesson?
4. What will be the best method of presenting the lesson?
5. Is the material in keeping with my objectives, is it meaningful?
6. Does this lesson fit logically and appropriately into the whole course?

STEPS IN PLANNING A GOOD LESSON

1. **Subject**--state just what this lesson is about.

2. **Objectives**--what do you wish to accomplish? Be specific.

3. **Materials**--What materials will you need for the lesson?

4. **Outline the subject matter**, listing references and other resources that are needed for the lesson.

5. State **how you will motivate or interest the group**, how you will explain the material, and how you will illustrate it in the lesson.

6. **List the questions or the procedure you will follow** in checking to see if the learner has gained a real understanding of the material.

7. Anticipate and **list the possible questions that the learner might ask** about the lesson.

8. List what points must be made in **summary** and how you will bring these out.

9. Plan to **explain the next lesson** and what the learner could do to prepare for it.

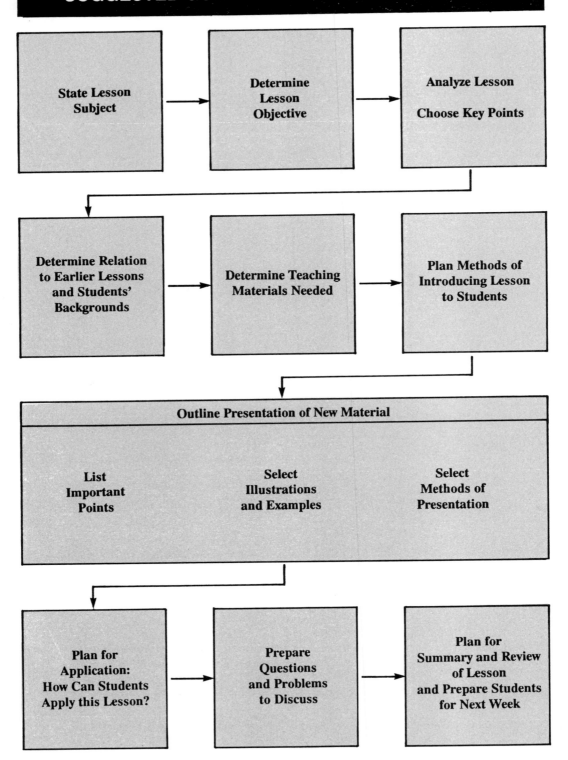

SUGGESTED GUIDE IN MAKING LESSON PLANS

State Lesson Subject → **Determine Lesson Objective** → **Analyze Lesson / Choose Key Points**

Determine Relation to Earlier Lessons and Students' Backgrounds → **Determine Teaching Materials Needed** → **Plan Methods of Introducing Lesson to Students**

Outline Presentation of New Material

List Important Points **Select Illustrations and Examples** **Select Methods of Presentation**

Plan for Application: How Can Students Apply this Lesson? → **Prepare Questions and Problems to Discuss** → **Plan for Summary and Review of Lesson and Prepare Students for Next Week**

146

TEACHER PRACTICE WORKSHEET III

My Lesson Plan

I. Objectives: (What do I want the learner to know or be able to do as a result of this lesson?)

_____

_____

II. Particular experiences, needs and interests of pupils that this lesson relates to:

_____

_____

III. My procedure for teaching this lesson:
    A. How I plan to begin

_____

_____

    B. Main points in the lesson (central ideas)
        1._____
        2._____
        3._____
    C. Main points of application (How can these ideas be applied to experience?)
        1._____
        2._____
        3._____
    D. What questions will help bring out and clarify main points?
        1._____
        2._____
        3._____
    E. How I plan to close (follow-up questions or activities):

_____

_____

IV. How I plan to encourage class participation:

_____

_____

V. How I plan to evaluate the success of this lesson:

_____

_____

VI. Materials needed for teaching this lesson:

_____

_____

_____

147

BEFORE THE CLASS OPENS

Preparing the Classroom

1. Be in your classroom ahead of time to greet the first students. Act as host.
2. Create a warm atmosphere.
3. Check the physical conditions--lighting, heating, ventilation.
4. Pre-arrange chairs in a circle to create a climate for discussion.
5. Arrange books, publications and materials needed.

Preparing the Learners

1. Put the learners at ease.
2. Find out what they already know.
3. Show them how and where the learning will help them.
4. Create a desire to learn.
5. Be enthusiastic.
6. Find out what interests and motivates them. This will double their interest.
7. Assure the learners of your sincere interest in them. Learn each student's name and use it often.

THE CLASS SESSION

Opening the Class

1. Start class on time.
2. Put group at ease.
3. Introduce self and members of the group.
4. Arouse interest. Have an "opener", a "starter", something to catch their interest.
5. Explain what the class is all about and how it will benefit them.

Teaching

1. **Have something new** to present at each session--something they would not want to miss.
2. **Select the best methods** for the particular situation, subject, objective, and group.
   1) Questions and Answers--good teaching is a matter of drawing out rather than a matter of putting in.
   2) Illustrations--teach by example, experience, parable or story.
   3) Discussion--centered around a genuine problem in atmosphere of openness to ideas of others.
   4) Explanations--clearly explain a point and/or have the student explain it.
   5) Case study--direct attention to a particular case or situation and consider how it might be dealt with.

6) Reports--presentation by a student to the class.
7) Bible games--may be fun as a review.
8) Review--from time to time, tie everything together.
9) Problem-Solving--work with students as they think through a problem.
10) Role Playing--spontaneous unrehearsed acting out of roles.
11) Projects--field trips, interviews, group activities.
12) Learning by Teaching--students prepare and teach a part of the class.

3. **Present step by step**, progressively. **Stress key points**.

4. **Be flexible.** Deal with the **learner's** questions and problems though this may mean postponing or changing your plan. While rationality and order characterize the planning of lessons, spontaneity and inspiration characterize the act of teaching.

5. **Refer to textbooks for corroboration and explanation.**

6. **Involve the learner.**

   1) Show how the learner can put information or skill to use.
   2) Provide opportunities for learners to participate.
   3) Commend good work.
   4) When the student doesn't understand
      - Never "put down" the student.
      - Find something to accept or build on. "That's an interesting idea."
      - Inquire as to reasons for the response. "Why do you think that?" "Why do you say that?" This will help you to help the student.
      - Make your comments constructive, positive and meaningful.
      - Be moderate in any correction and wind up with a pat on the back. This will pave the way for a desire to improve.

7. **Evaluation**

   1) Be sure the learner understands information. Don't try to cover too much. Material not understood by the learner is not learned.
   2) Ask questions, or have learners apply their understanding to particular situations.

8. **Summarizing**

   1) Summarize and emphasize main points you wish class to remember and utilize. Show how these will benefit them in their daily life.
   2) Make assignments for next time.
   3) Illustrate how this session is related to those coming up. Keep in mind interests of the group.
   4) Encourage attendance. Increase their confidence in the value of learning together.

TEACHING METHODS
USE OF QUESTIONS AND ANSWERS

1. Use of questions and answers should be based on the acknowledgment that the teacher can learn as much from the students as they can from the teacher.

2. Teacher and students join in a search for answers.

3. Use questions that encourage thinking; not a simple yes or no.

4. Kinds of Questions

   1) **Questions of Fact** (requiring a factual answer)

      Examples: What are the names of the 12 disciples?

      Who wrote the book of Acts?

   2) **Questions of Interpretation** (ask the student to interpret what the author <u>means</u>)

      - the meaning of a phrase
      - the meaning of a sentence
      - the meaning of some action
      - the meaning of the writer

      Examples: Why did Jesus cast the money changers out of the temple?

      Why did Rebekah prefer her son, Jacob, over his brother, Esau?

      Why was Jesus tempted by the devil?

      What does the Psalmist mean by "The Lord is my shepherd"?

   3) **Questions of Evaluation** (ask students to what extent the ideas under discussion have application to their own lives, their own personal experiences, and values).

      Questions of evaluation differ from interpretive questions in that they ask the students for their own viewpoints rather than asking them to interpret what the author means.

      Examples: What would you have done?

      If you had been Rebekah, would you have preferred Jacob?

      Would you have been able to reject the temptations if you had been Jesus? Why?

      Does it ever seem as if you are in a den of lions?

      What would you do?

5. Planning for Questions

   1) **Basic questions** (usually questions of interpretation)

      Starter questions with many implications such as: Why was Jesus tempted by the devil?

   2) **Follow-up questions**

      Possible questions to ask as follow-ups to the basic question (may be questions of interpretation, fact or evaluation)

   3) Ask one question at a time; double questions cause confusion

6. Use of **Hypothetical Questions**

   1) Ask student to place himself in a situation requiring him to face a problem and think through a solution

      Example: What do you do when one of your teachers at school seems dull and boring?

TEACHER PRACTICE WORKSHEET IV

Developing Questions

Select a citation from the Bible, a story or several verses.

Write reference here: _____

_____

Using this citation, write three questions of **fact**:

1. _____

2. _____

3. _____

Using this citation, write three questions of **interpretation**:

1. _____

2. _____

3. _____

Using this citation, write three questions of **evaluation**:

1. _____

2. _____

3. _____

Now select one of the questions as a **basic question** that might be used to lead off the discussion:

_____

_____

_____

_____

A CLASSIFICATION OF LEARNING EXPERIENCES
FROM MORE CONCRETE TO MORE ABSTRACT

Direct Personal Experiences
Practice
Teaching Others
Worksheets
Interviews
Projects
Problem Solving

Contrived Experiences
Role Playing
Games, Simulations
Trips
Discussion
Case Studies
Reports

Audio-Visual
Videos
Motion Pictures
Film Strips/Sound

Visual
Maps
Chalkboard
Diagrams
Pictures
Flannel Board

Audio
Lectures
Explanations
Story Telling
Recorded Tapes

Verbal Symbols
Books
Pamphlets
Written Materials

More Concrete

More Abstract

152

Teaching
the
Scriptures

Russell D. Robinson

New Edition
—revised and expanded—

TWELVE TEACHING METHODS

1. **Lecture** (explanation). Commonly used but difficult to use effectively; presents information in orderly way, but easy for student to turn off.

2. **Discussion**. Involves the student; people like to talk; discussion needs to center around a genuine problem or common concern that seems important and relevant; teacher (as well as the students) must have searching attitude.

3. **Story Telling**. Commonly used method in teaching younger children; know the story well and in the telling make it come to life.

4. **Role Playing**. A brief, spontaneous, unrehearsed presentation of a problem or a situation in which certain class members act out certain roles; children regularly role play: play house, play school, etc.; role playing followed by discussion.

5. **Special Projects**. Learning by doing; conducting interviews (with church workers, other parents, businessmen, career women, etc.); taking field trips (to another church, special services, church library or reading room, etc.; either as group assignments or individual assignments.

6. **Problem-Solving** (hypothetical questions, case studies, current events). Discussion of a problem and its solution in the light of the Bible.

7. **Reports**. Bringing reports back to class of work done outside of class.

8. **Bible Games**. Contrived situations or games, or perhaps games patterned after TV shows.

9. **Review**. Systematic review of main points dealt with over a period of time.

10. **Illustration** (parables, examples). Use of illustrations from personal experience, or from religious periodicals to show application.

11. **Learning by Teaching**. Pupils helping other pupils to learn; practice in planning and teaching six-minute segments to their class or another class. Seneca wrote, "He who teaches learns twice."

12. **Extra-Sunday School Activities** (outside of class hour). Learning outside of the Sunday School hour through attendance at church inspiration meetings, special events such as lectures, films, youth programs, etc.

CONDITIONS FOR LEARNING

1. **Instructional climate and attitude toward learning**

    1) According to Robert Mager, the purpose of all instruction should be "to send students away from instruction with at least as favorable an attitude toward the subject taught as they had when they first arrived." The key to accomplishing this attitude toward learning is instructional climate.

    2) How? Accentuate positive conditions and consequences and eliminate the negative aversive conditions and consequences.

2. **Aversive conditions which create a negative climate for learning**

    1) Conditions which cause fear and anxiety, distress, tension, foreboding, worry or disquiet, anticipation of the unpleasant.

    2) Conditions which cause frustration, blocking or interfering with desire to learn.

    3) Conditions which cause humiliation and embarrassment, causing a lowering of a person's self-respect and self-esteem, making the student uncomfortable or self-conscious or feeling shamed, debased or degraded.

    4) Conditions which cause boredom.

3. **Positive conditions which create a favorable climate for learning**

    1) Acknowledging students' responses, whether correct or incorrect, as attempts to learn and following them with accepting rather than rejecting comments.

    2) Providing instruction in increments that will allow success most of the time.

    3) Providing enough sign posts so that students always know where they are and where they are expected to go.

    4) Giving the student some choice in selecting and sequencing the subject matter.

    5) Relating new information to old, within the experience of the student.

    6) Treating the student as a person.

    7) Providing instructional tasks that are relevant to your objectives and letting your student know what the objectives are.

    8) Providing opportunity for a high degree of student participation.

154

PREPARATION FOR ASSIGNMENTS

The presentation of questions and/or citations to students by means of written assignments is a well known and successful practice. Assignments pay high dividends in terms of efficient teaching and effective learning with economy of time for both the teacher and student.

1. **Home Assignments may be done in many ways**.
   1) May be given out in class; mailed; telephoned.
   2) May be made for the class as a whole; specific for individual pupils; or both.
   3) Should complement and supplement class work.

2. **Analyze your assignments**:
   1) Is each assignment essentially like the previous one?
   2) Do parents have to do most of the assignment for their children?
   3) Are the questions too long? too hard? too vague?
   4) Do your pupils understand the words they find in these assignments?
   5) Is there too much emphasis on the letter and not enough on the spirit?
   6) How do pupils respond?
   7) Are you evaluating the pupil's answers in class to determine whether the assignments are too easy or too difficult or uninteresting?
   8) Do you always have the same number of questions requiring the same type of response or is there variety?
   9) Do questions require a simple yes or no? Or do they require a student to think through his/her response?
   10) Are the assignments really necessary?
   11) Do you consider individual needs in assigning useful lessons?

3. **Many possibilities in types of assignments.**
   1) The more creative and varied, the more interesting.

4. **Tips in writing assignments**:
   1) The information should be presented in a direct, concise, factual manner and in logical sequence.
   2) The language should be carefully chosen to suit the reading vocabulary of those for whom the assignments are intended.
   3) The references and questions should be well arranged and spaced. The material should not be crowded. The general arrangement should make it easy to follow.
   4) Discrimination in the choice of material to be included should be exercised.
   5) Assignment sheets should be reproduced by some method which will result in attractive, neat, legible copy.

5. **Assignments should be used**.
   1) Assignments should be referred to and analyzed in class, even if students have not come prepared.

TEACHER PRACTICE WORKSHEET V

Preparing an Assignment

Date

_____

Subject of Lesson

_____

Introduction (A brief statement of the subject)

_____

_____

_____

Content (Citations for student to study or task to be performed)

_____

_____

_____

Questions (To cause the student to read carefully and apply what he has learned.)

_____

_____

_____

_____

Personal Note (Encouragement, support, or compliment to student when appropriate.)

_____

_____

_____

TEACHER PRACTICE WORKSHEET VI

For Teacher Discussion: Thinking About Sunday School

Please complete these sentences. Then share, compare, and discuss your responses.

1. Sunday School is important because _____

_____

_____

2. The reason I teach Sunday School is _____

_____

_____

3. Teaching Sunday School today is different because _____

_____

_____

_____

4. What I remember most from my own Sunday School training is _____

_____

_____

_____

5. My goal in teaching Sunday School is _____

_____

_____

_____

TEACHER PRACTICE WORKSHEET VII

For Teacher Discussion: Thinking About the Bible

Please complete these sentences. Then share, compare, and discuss your responses.

1. The Bible is important because _____

_____

_____

2. People read and study the Bible in order to _____

_____

3. What I find difficult in teaching the Bible is _____

_____

4. What I find most helpful in teaching the Bible is _____

_____

_____

5. My goal in Bible teaching is _____

_____

_____

6. When I turn to the Bible for inspiration, I am most likely to turn to _____

_____

Why?_____

_____

7. What has helped me most in learning more about the Bible is _____

_____

158

TEACHER PRACTICE WORKSHEET VIII

For Teacher Discussion: Thinking About Teaching

Please complete these sentences. Then share, compare, and discuss your responses.

1. What I liked most about my favorite Sunday School teacher was _____

_____

_____

2. When I am talking, I feel _____

_____

_____

3. When students talk, I _____

_____

_____

4. I feel annoyed when students _____

_____

_____

5. I feel good when students _____

_____

_____

6. When a student assumes leadership of the class, I feel _____

_____

_____

7. Pupils learn best when _____

_____

TEACHER PRACTICE WORKSHEET IX

For Teacher Discussion: Jesus as Teacher (Master)

Read the account of Jesus teaching Nicodemus, John 3:1-21
How did Jesus use various teaching methods in teaching Nicodemus?
Find examples of the following methods from this account.

Discussion _____

_____

_____

Questions and Answers _____

_____

_____

_____

Illustrations or Examples _____

_____

_____

_____

Use of Scriptures _____

_____

_____

Explanations or Lecture _____

_____

_____

_____

Use of Humor _____

TEACHER PRACTICE WORKSHEET X

For Teachers to Practice Teaching a Bible Lesson

Select a story or passage from the Bible._____

Now, plan a five minute class segment in which you would teach this passage.

What will be your objective (aim) in teaching this passage?

_____

What major points will you emphasize?_____

_____

_____

_____

How will you apply the Bible lesson to today?_____

_____

How will you involve the learners?_____

_____

How will you start?_____

_____

What questions or other teaching methods will you use?_____

_____

_____

_____

What books or other materials will you need?_____

_____

Now teach your five minutes to 3 or 4 other teachers who will be your "pupils". Let them know the "age" you are teaching.

161

NOTES

APPENDIX IV

BIBLE STUDY WORKSHEETS

"Indeed everything that was written long ago in the scriptures was meant to teach us something about hope from the examples scripture gives of how people who did not give up were helped by God."

Romans 15:4
Jerusalem Bible

Bible study worksheets

Following are 34 Bible study worksheets. They are not intended to cover all or even most of the Scriptures but to be examples of approaches that can be taken in an in-depth study. The worksheets can be used by individuals studying alone or by Bible study groups and may be used as models for developing more worksheets. The worksheets included are designed for and have been used by adults in my classes, but could be simplified and adapted for use by youth.

BIBLE STUDY WORKSHEET I

STUDYING THE BIBLE

Please complete these sentences. Then share, compare, and discuss your responses.

1. Studying the Bible is important because _____

_____

_____

2. People read and study the Bible in order to _____

_____

_____

3. What helps me most in studying the Bible is _____

_____

_____

4. One of my favorite Bible stories is _____

What makes it my favorite is _____

_____

_____

5. My least favorite part of the Bible is _____

6. When I turn to the Bible for inspiration, I am most likely to turn to _____

_____

Why? _____

_____

7. My goals in Bible study are _____

_____

_____

BIBLE STUDY WORKSHEET II

A CHRONOLOGY OF THE BIBLE

Before Abraham:

[ ]

2000-1500 B.C. Abraham to Moses:

[ ]

1500-1000 B.C. Moses to David:

[ ]

1000-500 B.C. David to Daniel:

[ ]

500-0 B.C. Daniel to Jesus:

[ ]

0-100 B.C. Jesus and Early Christianity:

[ ]

Locate these Bible characters by numbers in the appropriate chronological boxes on the left.

1. Ezekiel
2. Malachi
3. Zechariah
4. Peter
5. Haggai
6. Obadiah
7. Noah
8. James
9. Jacob-Israel
10. Titus
11. Jonah
12. Isaiah
13. Jeremiah
14. Phillip
15. Zerubbabel
16. Amos
17. Elijah
18. Stephen
19. John
20. Gideon
21. Joshua
22. Nahum
23. Paul
24. Hosea
25. Ruth
26. Micah
27. Ezra
28. Nehemiah
29. Samson
30. Luke
31. Isaac
32. Saul
33. Samuel
34. Elisha
35. Timothy
36. Esther
37. Jehoshaphat
38. Deborah

BIBLE STUDY WORKSHEET III

LITERATURE OF THE BIBLE

Mark the correct number in the blank. Some have more than one answer.

_____ Poetry	1. Isaiah
	2. Galatians
_____ Drama	3. Ruth
	4. Leviticus
_____ Short Story	5. Psalms
	6. Mark
_____ Laws	7. Genesis
	8. I, II Kings
_____ Songs	9. Job
	10. I, II Timothy
_____ History of a New Church	11. I, II Samuel
	12. Esther
_____ Story of Joseph	13. Acts
	14. Revelation
_____ Biography	15. Song of Solomon
	16. Proverbs
_____ Letter to Churches	17. Amos
	18. Micah
_____ Letter to Individual	19. Exodus
	20. Jeremiah
_____ Autobiography	21. Matthew
	22. Philippians
_____ Visions	23. Nehemiah
_____ Wise Sayings	
_____ Letter to a Church	
_____ History of Kingdoms	
_____ History of Resettlement and Rebuilding	

BIBLE STUDY WORKSHEET IV

BIBLE COMMENTARIES AND DICTIONARIES

Review three passages of Scripture. Then look these up in a **Bible dictionary** and a **Bible commentary** and see what these say about the passages.

Write down any new ideas you discover about each passage.

In commentary look up Matthew 5:3,4,5

In dictionary look up "beatitudes"

_____

_____

_____

_____

In commentary look up II Kings 6:8-17

In dictionary look up "Elisha"

_____

_____

_____

_____

In commentary look up Acts 18:1-5

In dictionary look up"Paul", "Aquila"

_____

_____

_____

_____

BIBLE STUDY WORKSHEET V

BIBLE TRANSLATIONS

Read Galatians 5:7-10 in the King James Version.

Now read the same passage in <u>three</u> modern translations (such as Revised Standard Version, Phillips Modern English, New English, Good News, New International, Amplified, etc.)

Did the modern translation clarify the meaning?_____

_____

In what way?_____

_____

_____

_____

_____

Did you prefer one translation over another?_____

Which one?_____ Why?_____

_____

_____

_____

_____

Now do the same with these citations:

      Ephesians 4:16   II Timothy 3:14-17
      Galatians 5:19-23   Exodus 20:3-17
      Mark 1:14, 15   Psalms 23:1-6

It is sometimes said that the best Bible commentary is another translation. Why?

_____

BIBLE STUDY WORKSHEET VI

COMPARE BIBLE COMMENTARIES

Review Scriptural passage Matthew 6:9-13 (The Lord's Prayer). Look up the passage (by chapter and verse) in two different Bible Commentaries (such as Dummelow's or Peake's).

What did you learn?_____

_____

_____

_____

_____

How do the commentaries differ?_____

_____

_____

_____

Which commentary did you find easier to read and understand?_____

_____

Why?_____

_____

_____

Were there statements that you disagreed with?_____

Why?_____

_____

Now do the same thing with Nehemiah, Chapters 2, 4 and 6.

BIBLE STUDY WORKSHEET VII

COMPARE BIBLE DICTIONARIES

Look up the same word in two different Bible dictionaries (such as <u>New Westminster Bible Dictionary</u> or <u>Harper's Bible Dictionary</u>).

      Canaan

      Joseph

      Shewbread

      Miracles

      Kings

      Parables

How did the dictionaries differ? _____

_____

_____

_____

How were the dictionaries similar? _____

_____

_____

_____

What did you learn from the information given? _____

_____

_____

Which dictionary did you find easier to read and understand? _____

Why? _____

_____

BIBLE STUDY WORKSHEET VIII

USING A CONCORDANCE LEXICON

Comprehensive Bible concordances (such as <u>Strong's Exhaustive Concordance</u> and <u>Young's Analytical Concordance</u>) contain concise Hebrew and Greek lexicons so Bible readers can easily look up meanings of the original Hebrew or Greek words. In Strong's, the lexicons are in the back of the book by <u>number</u> which appears in the concordance itself with every use of a particular word. You can quickly go from a word you wish to study in a Bible verse to the concordance listing of that word. The reference to the word will list a number and then you turn to the lexicon for a definition of its use and meaning. Do this with several words in a verse and you can make your own translation! Young's Analytical is similar, except for the numbers system, as the words and brief definitions are in the body of the concordance itself.

Look up Psalm 32:2. Suppose you want to find the meaning of "man" in that verse. Now look up "man" in Strong's concordance and find Psalm 32:2 in the list of the use of "man". You will find the number <u>120</u> following the reference to Psalm 32:2. Now look for number 120 in the Hebrew lexicon. Note the Hebrew word "adam" translated "man" means a human being, mankind, an individual, a person. So Psalm 32:2 could have been translated "Blessed is the <u>one</u> unto whom" or "Blessed is the <u>person</u> unto whom...", etc.

Now take John 1:14-17. You want an understanding of the meaning of "grace". Look up "grace" in Strong's concordance. What number is given?_____ Look up the number (5485) in the Greek lexicon. What does it say about grace?

_____

_____

_____

_____

How does this help you to understand John's use of the word "grace" in referring to Jesus?

_____

_____

_____

_____

_____

BIBLE STUDY WORKSHEET IX

USING A REFERENCE BIBLE

Use a Reference Bible. It will have a column of references to related Bible citations in a column down the center of each page or sometimes as two columns on each side or as footnotes at the bottom of the page. Look up the Gospel of John, Chapter 1:1-28. Read these verses. Now note the references given for related citations and look up these. Words most likely to be referenced will be **Word, beginning, light, glory, grace**. Also the names **John, Elias (Elijah), Prophet**. Note for verse 23 the reference gives the Old Testament Scripture being quoted by John. How did the references to other citations expand your information or understanding of the passage? Give some examples.

Word:_____

_____

Beginning:_____

_____

Light:_____

_____

Glory:_____

_____

Grace:_____

_____

John:_____

_____

Elias:_____

_____

Prophet:_____

_____

BIBLE STUDY WORKSHEET X

ANCIENT PEOPLES

Though there have been throughout history massive shifts of peoples, inter-mixing of populations, deportations, and changing boundaries, yet peoples and their identities persist. Using a Bible dictionary and Bible atlas, look up the history of the peoples below. Can you find other names by which the peoples were known? What were their main cities? What is the modern name for their location?

Ancient Name	Other Names/Major Cities	Modern Name/Location
Amalekites		
Amorites		
Ammonites		
Assyrians		
Babylonians/Chaldeans		
Canaanites		
Edom/Idumeans		
Egyptians		
Hittites		
Medians/Medes		
Mesopotamians		
Midian/Midianites		
Moab/Moabites		
Persia/Persians		
Philistines		
Phoenicians		
Sidon/Zidonians		
Syria/Syrians		

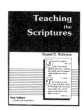

BIBLE STUDY WORKSHEET XI

GENESIS 1, 2, 3, 4

Some six hundred years elapsed between the writing of Gen. 1:1--2:3 and Gen. 2:4--4:26. The accounts in Chapters 2, 3, 4 were the earliest to be written, centuries before Chapter 1.

Study, contrast and compare the main ideas expressed in the two accounts:

Gen. 1:1--2:3	Gen. 2:4--4:26
1:1-5	2:4-6
1:6-8	2:7
1:9-13	2:8-17
1:14-19	2:18--3:7
1:20-23	3:8-15
1:24-31	3:16-24
2:1-3	4:1-26

Scholars agree that the Genesis 1 is "more spiritual" in the concept of God and man. Why?

_____

_____

Why would the Bible editors in 400 B.C. who wrote the Genesis 1 account have left in the earlier second story of creation which contradicts their opening account?

_____

_____

_____

BIBLE STUDY WORKSHEET XII

NOAH

The ancient story of Noah (Gen. 6-10) and the flood was told and retold to illustrate that God is just, that those who are just and righteous and obey God shall prosper and be protected.

What does the story tell us about Noah? _____

_____

_____

_____

What might the symbols of the ark and the flood mean? _____

_____

_____

_____

What might the raven and dove symbolize? _____

_____

_____

_____

What is God's covenant with Noah? _____

_____

_____

_____

The sons of Noah represent the peoples of the time. What peoples did Shem, Ham and

Japheth and their sons represent? _____

_____

_____

BIBLE STUDY WORKSHEET XIII

JOB

Job challenges the view that the evil that came to him was the result of his unrighteousness. He proclaims his innocence as his "friends" conduct a trial to prove him guilty.

How do we know that Job is innocent? (chapter 1)_____

_____

_____

_____

What do his friends accuse him of? (chapters 3-28)_____

_____

_____

_____

How would you characterize Job's direct appeal to God? (chapter 29-31)_____

_____

_____

_____

How does God respond? (chapter 38-41)_____

_____

_____

_____

How do we know that Job was right in maintaining his innocence and appealing directly to

God? (chapter 42)_____

_____

_____

BIBLE STUDY WORKSHEET XIV

PICK A PATRIARCH

Select one of the following patriarchs: Abraham (Gen. 12-22), Isaac (Gen. 24, 26), Jacob (Gen. 25-35), Joseph (Gen. 37-46).

Select one incident from the life of the patriarch: _____

_____

Respond to these questions:

What qualities or attributes of God did this patriarch express? _____

_____

_____

What un-God-like qualities did he (or others) express in the incident?

_____

_____

How was the person changed by the experience? _____

_____

_____

What brought about the change in him? _____

_____

What can we learn from this person's experience? _____

_____

_____

Any modern day examples or illustrations? _____

_____

_____

Now, try another incident and/or another patriarch.

BIBLE STUDY WORKSHEET XV

THE TEN COMMANDMENTS

Select one of the Ten Commandments (Ex. 20:1-17):_____

Rewrite the Commandment using your own words:_____

_____

What does this Commandment mean to you?_____

_____

_____

_____

_____

Now, how would you apply this Commandment to a particular situation or circumstance?

_____

_____

_____

_____

_____

How would you share its meaning with another person?_____

_____

_____

Can you think of or find any other "laws" in Exodus, Leviticus, or Deuteronomy that you think

might be considered an expansion of this Commandment?_____

_____

_____

179

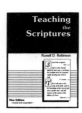

SAMUEL, SAUL, DAVID

1. Compare and describe the prayers of Hannah in I Samuel 1:12-17 and I Samuel 2:1-10:

   _____

   _____

2. Describe the situation at the Tabernacle of the Lord (I Samuel 2:11-26)

   _____

   _____

3. What did Samuel warn the people that a king could do to them? (I Samuel 8:1-22)

   _____

   _____

4. Why did Samuel secretly anoint David while Saul was still king? (I Samuel Chs. 15, 16)

   _____

   _____

5. Describe David's friendship with Jonathan (I Samuel 20). What does this teach us about

   friendship?_____

   _____

6. Though Saul would gladly have killed David, and pursued him for this purpose, David

   twice spared Saul (I Samuel 24 and 26). Why?_____

   _____

7. What can we learn from the story of David, Nabal and Abigail? (I Samuel 25)

   _____

8. What was Saul's fatal mistake? (I Samuel 28:1-25)_____

   _____

POETRY OF THE BIBLE

Hebrew poetry uses parallelism rather than meter for rhythm, and repetition rather than rhyme. The first line presents the thought, and the second reiterates it, adds to it, or contrasts it.

<u>Find two examples in Psalms</u>:

1. _____

_____

2. _____

_____

<u>Find two examples in Proverbs</u>:

1. _____

_____

2. _____

_____

<u>Write your own two line psalm or proverb using parallelism</u>:

_____

_____

_____

_____

_____

_____

_____

_____

BIBLE STUDY WORKSHEET XVIII

MONARCHY AND DIVIDED KINGDOM

1. Why did David make Jerusalem his capitol after he had reunited north and south? (II Samuel 5:1-12)_____

2. Why was David not permitted to build a temple for the ark that he had brought to Jerusalem? (II Samuel 7:1-17)_____

3. How did the prophet Nathan rebuke King David for his affair with Bathsheba? (II Samuel 12:1-10)_____

4. Solomon had a reputation for wisdom, but his wealth, fame, trading, and foreign wives led to his worship of other gods (I Kings 11:1-10). Look up in a Bible dictionary Ashtoreth, Milcom, Chemosh, Molech. What were the gods like?

_____

5. After Solomon's death his son Rehoboam became king. Why did the kingdom split in two? (I Kings 12:1-24)_____

6. The northern kingdom called Israel began with Jeroboam as first king. What does a Bible dictionary say about the golden calves at Dan and Bethel? (I Kings 12:25-33)

_____

7. In its 200 years of existence Israel was ruled by nine different dynasties and nineteen kings, seven of whom were assassinated. Which king made Samaria the capitol? (I Kings 16:21-24)

_____

8. Describe the confrontation between Elijah and the Baalite prophets at Mount Carmel (I Kings 18:16-39)_____

9. What happened after Elijah heard the "still small voice"? (I Kings 19:11-21)

_____

10. The southern kingdom of Judah began with Rehoboam as king. All his successors were also of the line of David. Two kings of Judah whose reigns were 200 years apart were Jehoshaphat (I Kings 22:41-46; II Chronicles 17:1-10) and Josiah (II Kings 22:1-20; II Chronicles 34:1-33). Why are they among those called "reform kings"?_____

_____

11. The northern kingdom of Israel fell to the _____ Empire in 721 B.C.

12. One hundred thirty five years later the southern kingdom of Judah fell to the _____ Empire in 586 B.C.

BIBLE STUDY WORKSHEET XIX

THE PROPHETIC MESSAGES

Select any one of the books of the prophets. See if you can find examples in that prophet's writings that emphasize any of the following teachings (not every prophet wrote on all of these points):

<u>Write in numbers of chapters and verses.</u>

1. God is the one Lord over all._____

_____

2. The worship of false gods is denounced._____

_____

3. Animal sacrifice and ritual observance denounced._____

_____

4. Breaking of social obligations to the poor, to widows, to orphans is denounced.

_____

5. Israel's enemies and problems are a result of Israel's sins._____

_____

6. The Day of the Lord (Day of Judgment) is near._____

_____

7. A remnant will endure._____

_____

8. A Messiah is expected._____

_____

Now try this with another prophet's writings.

183

BIBLE STUDY WORKSHEET XX

MICAH AND ISAIAH

1. What sins did Micah denounce? (Micah 2, 3)_____
_____
_____

2. Where was the Messiah to be born? What blessings would he bring to the people ? (Micah 5)_____
_____

3. What does the Lord require? (Micah 6) _____
_____
_____
_____

4. What was Isaiah's experience when he entered the Temple? (Isaiah 6:1-13)
_____
_____

5. What was the message Isaiah had to give?_____
_____
_____
_____

6. When Hezekiah was sick, what did he do? (II Kings 20:1-11, Isaiah 38:1-20).
_____
_____
_____

7. What was Isaiah's response after Hezekiah showed the treasury to the envoy? (II Kings 20:16-18)_____
_____
_____

8. Describe the Messiah as he is described in Isaiah, chapters 9, 11, and 12.
_____
_____
_____

9. Summarize the leading thought Isaiah expresses in Isaiah, chapters 32 and 35.
_____
_____
_____

BIBLE STUDY WORKSHEET XXI

AMOS AND HOSEA

1. Where did Amos live?_____

2. Why did Amos denounce the sins of Israel's neighbors? (Amos 1:3, 6, 9, 11; 2:1, 4)
_____
_____
_____

3. How were the Children of Israel disobeying the Commandments and moral law? (Amos 2:6-8)
_____
_____

4. What did Amos predict would happen to Israel? (Amos 8:4-13)_____
_____
_____

5. What symbolism did Hosea use to warn Israel of the impending crisis? (Hosea 2)
_____
_____

6. What do the names of Hosea's three children mean? (Hosea 1:4, 6, 9)

　　　Jezreel_____

　　　Lo-ruhamah_____

　　　Lo-ammi_____

7. How does Hosea 2:21-23 compare with these names? What does it mean?
_____
_____
_____

8. What did God say was the cause of Israel's defection? (Hosea 2:8; 4:6, 10-14; 8:7)
_____
_____
_____

9. What is necessary for redemption? (Hosea 2:19; 10:12; 13:4-9; 14:8)
_____
_____
_____

Teaching
the
Scriptures

Russell D. Robinson

New Edition
— revised and expanded •

BIBLE STUDY WORKSHEET XXII

JOEL, JONAH, ZEPHANIAH, HABAKKUK

1. What does Joel say about the mercy of the Lord? (Joel 2:12-27)

_____

_____

2. What is the lesson that Jonah learned? (Jonah Chs. 3 and 4)

_____

_____

3. Why was the book of Jonah considered a "protest" book against Ezra's policies?

(Ezra 10:1-17)_____

_____

4. Summarize what Zephaniah says of the Day of the Lord in Chapter 1.

_____

_____

5. Summarize what Zephaniah says of Jerusalem's sin and redemption in Chapter 3.

_____

_____

6. What was it that disturbed Habakkuk so deeply? (Habakkuk 1)

_____

_____

7. What, in short, did Habakkuk say in his prayer? (Habakkuk 3).

_____

_____

_____

BIBLE STUDY WORKSHEET XXIII

JEREMIAH

1. Describe Jeremiah's commission. (Jeremiah 1:1-10) _____

_____

2. What is the lesson from the potter working the clay? (Jeremiah 18:1-6) _____

_____

3. How were the children of Judah unfaithful to the Mt. Sinai covenant? (Jeremiah 7:1-20,

11:1-13 _____

_____

4. What did Jeremiah warn would happen? (Jeremiah 12:14-17) _____

_____

5. What did Jeremiah say of the return of the remnant? (Jeremiah 23:1-8)_____

_____

6. What was the lesson from the good and bad figs? (Jeremiah 24)_____

_____

7. How does chapter 34 show that Judah was beyond repentance?_____

_____

8. What was the lesson to be learned from the Rechabites? (Jeremiah 35)_____

_____

_____

9. Describe the fall of Jerusalem and the destruction of the temple. (Jeremiah 52:12-28)

and its impact on the people. (Lamentations Ch. 1)_____

_____

_____

BIBLE STUDY WORKSHEET XXIV

EZEKIEL AND II ISAIAH

1. Describe the call of Ezekiel. (Ezekiel 2) _____

_____

_____

2. What is Ezekiel's role as a watchman? (Ezekiel 3:16-21)_____

_____

_____

3. What is his message to the righteous? (Compare Ezekiel 3:16-21 with 18:1-20)_____

_____

_____

4. What does Ezekiel say about God as Shepherd? (Ezekiel 34:11-31)_____

_____

5. In what ways was Isaiah 40 a message of comfort?_____

_____

6. How did Isaiah describe the making of an idol? (Isaiah 41:7; 44:9-13)_____

_____

7. How is God described as Redeemer? (Isaiah 43)_____

_____

8. How does Isaiah describe the "suffering servant" (Messiah)? (Isaiah 52:13--53:12)_____

_____

9. How does Isaiah describe "the woman" (Israel)? (Isaiah 54)_____

_____

BIBLE STUDY WORKSHEET XXV

HAGGAI, ZECHARIAH, MALACHI

1. According to Haggai what relationship was there between the unfinished temple and the

unhappy lives of the people of Judah? _____

_____

_____

2. What was the central message of Zechariah? (Zechariah 1:1-6) _____

_____

_____

3. Describe the vision of the candlestick and the two olive trees. (Zechariah 4) _____

_____

_____

4. What did Zechariah see for the restoration of Jerusalem? (Zechariah 8) _____

_____

_____

5. List the reasons why Malachi rebuked the Jews generally, and the priests in particular.

(Malachi 1 and 2) _____

_____

_____

_____

6. Contrast Malachi's description of the forerunner of the Messiah and the Messiah

himself. (Malachi 3:1-5; 4:1-6) _____

_____

BIBLE STUDY WORKSHEET XXVI

NEHEMIAH

Read Nehemiah Chapters 2, 4, 6.

1. Why did Nehemiah need the Persian king's permission to rebuild the wall?_____

_____

2. How does the king respond to Nehemiah's request?_____

_____

3. How did the people of Jerusalem respond to Nehemiah's mission?_____

_____

_____

4. Who were Nehemiah's enemies?_____

Why?_____

_____

5. How did Nehemiah reply to their scoffing and threats?_____

_____

_____

6. How would you describe the enemy strategies to stop the work?_____

_____

_____

7. How did Nehemiah respond to further plots?_____

_____

8. How can we apply this story of Nehemiah to our experience today?_____

_____

_____

THE PROPHETS WERE POETS

Hebrew poetry uses parallelism rather than meter for rhythm, and repetition rather than rhyme. The first line presents the thought, and the second line reiterates it, adds to it, or contrasts it. [The Revised Standard Version, and some other versions print lines as poetry.]

<u>Find two examples in Isaiah 1, 2, 3:</u>

1._____

_____

2._____

_____

<u>Find two examples in Jeremiah 5, 6:</u>

1._____

_____

2._____

_____

<u>Find two examples in Micah 5, 6, 7:</u>

1._____

_____

2._____

_____

<u>Find two examples in Isaiah 40, 41, 42:</u>

1._____

_____

2._____

_____

BIBLE STUDY WORKSHEET XXVIII

COMPARING THE GOSPELS

Select one of the following Gospel stories and compare the authors' accounts of the story:

	Matthew	Mark	Luke	John
John the Baptist	3:1-12	1:1-8	3:1-20	1:19-28
Baptism of Jesus	3:13-17	1:9-11	3:21,22	1:29-34
Temptation of Jesus	4:1-11	1:12,13	4:1-13	--
Healing Peter's wife's mother	8:14-17	1:29-32	4:38-41	--
Healing of Palsied Man	9:1-8	2:1-12	5:17-26	--
Feeding of 5,000	14:13-23	6:30-46	9:10-17	6:1-15
Walking on Water	14:24-36	6:47-56	--	6:16-21
Peter's Reply to Jesus	16:13-20	8:27-30	9:18-21	--

In what ways are the stories the same?

_____

_____

_____

_____

In what ways do the stories differ?

_____

_____

_____

_____

Which of the accounts did you prefer?_____

Why?_____

_____

BIBLE STUDY WORKSHEET XXIX

SERMON ON THE MOUNT

The Sermon on the Mount is considered by scholars to be a collection of Jesus' teachings on the kingdom of heaven (translation: "reign and rule of God"). The kingdom of heaven, Jesus said, was "at hand"--which can be translated "is come", "has arrived", "is near", "is here." Some scholars believe the sermon is constructed with seven points or concepts about citizenship in the kingdom. In your own words summarize the central idea of each of the main points.

Matthew 5:1-12 _____
_____
_____
_____

Matthew 5:13 _____
_____
_____
_____

Matthew 5:14-16 _____
_____
_____
_____

Matthew 5:17-48 _____
_____
_____
_____

Matthew 6:1-18 _____
_____
_____
_____

Matthew 6:19-34 _____
_____
_____
_____

Matthew 7:1-27 _____
_____
_____
_____

BIBLE STUDY WORKSHEET XXX

STORY OF STEPHEN

Read chapters 6 and 7 in the book of Acts.

Discuss the following:

Stephen's position in the Church:_____
_____
_____
_____

The circumstances of his arrest:_____
_____
_____
_____

His defense before the Council:_____
_____
_____
_____

His use of the Scriptures:_____
_____
_____
_____
_____
_____
_____

The response of the Council to his defense:_____
_____
_____
_____

Stephen's response to their condemnation and stoning:_____
_____
_____
_____

What can we learn from Stephen's experience?_____
_____
_____
_____
_____

BIBLE STUDY WORKSHEET XXXI

PAUL'S LETTERS

Read one of Paul's letters such as Philippians, Colossians, or I Thessalonians.

Discuss the following:

Paul's purpose in writing:_____

_____

_____

What major points does Paul make in the letter?_____

_____

_____

_____

What evidence of Paul's personal interest in church workers?_____

_____

_____

_____

_____

Would you have saved this letter and read and re-read it so that it would come to be regarded as Scripture?_____

Why?_____

_____

_____

Why do you think Paul was an effective teacher?_____

_____

_____

BIBLE STUDY WORKSHEET XXXII

REVELATION

The book of Revelation is filled with dramatic imagery and symbols, most of which are taken directly from the Old Testament in 278 of the 404 verses in Revelation. The reader, knowing the Old Testament, could "decode" the apocalypse. What might each symbol below mean?

<u>Revelation</u>

1:12   seven golden candlesticks (Zechariah 4:2)_____

1:13   son of man (Daniel 7:13)_____

2:20   Jezebel (I Kings 21:25,26)_____

4:6   four beasts (living creatures) (Ezekiel 1:5,10)_____

5:6   Lamb (Isaiah 53:7)_____

6:4   red horse (Zechariah 6:2,3)_____

8:3   golden censer (Leviticus 16:12,13)_____

8:11   wormwood (Jeremiah 9:15)_____

10:2   little book (Ezekiel 2:9,10; 3:1-3)_____

11:4   two olive trees (Zechariah 4:11-14)_____

12:1   woman (Isaiah 54:1-17; 66:7)_____

12:3   dragon with ten horns (Daniel 7:24-27)_____

12:17   dragon vs. woman (Genesis 3:15)_____

14:8   Babylon (Jeremiah 51:6-13)_____

21:1   new heaven and earth (Isaiah 65:17,18)_____

21:2   holy city (Isaiah 52:1)_____

22:1   pure river (Ezekiel 47:6-12)_____

22:2   tree of Life (Psalms 1:3; Isaiah 65:22)_____

Do you see that the book of Revelation was not intended to be obscure, mysterious or confusing to its readers who were familiar with images echoed from the older Scriptures and could "translate" the book into a powerful message of the certain triumph of good over evil?

BIBLE STUDY WORKSHEET XXXIII

EARLY CHRISTIANITY

1. Describe early Christian groups. How did they function? How were they organized?

    _____

    _____

    _____

    _____

2. Describe meetings the early Christians held:
    Sundays_____

    _____

    Weekdays_____

    _____

3. Describe the roles of early Christian workers. Any individual might perform several of these roles:
    Apostles_____
    Prophets_____
    Teachers_____
    Evangelists_____
    Elders_____
    Readers_____
    Pastors_____
    Bishops (overseers)_____
    Deacons (assistants)_____

4. How did early Christians live their commitment to the risen Christ?

    _____

    _____

    _____

    _____

    _____

5. During the first century the Christian Bible was _____

    _____

    _____

    _____

6. In what ways are Christian churches today different from these early groups?

    _____

    _____

    _____

    _____

    _____

BIBLE STUDY WORKSHEET XXXIV

CHRISTIANITY TODAY

Please complete these sentences. Then share, compare, and discuss your responses.

1. Christianity has given the world_____

_____

2. If Jesus were to return today, he would say to the Christian church_____

_____

_____

3. The difference between Christian religion and Christian practice is_____

_____

_____

4. Christianity's saddest hour was_____

_____

5. Throughout Christian history the Bible has been_____

_____

6. Christianity's brightest moments have been_____

_____

_____

7. The future spread of Christianity depends upon_____

_____

_____

8. If I were arrested today and accused of being a Christian, the evidence for

conviction would be_____

_____

NOTES

INDEX

Consider the incredible love that the Father has shown us in allowing us to be called "children of God"--and that is not just what we are called, but what we _are_. Our heredity on the God-ward side is no mere figure of speech--which explains why the world will no more recognise us than it recognised Christ. Oh, dear children of mine (forgive the affection of an old man!), have you realised it? Here and now we are God's children. We don't know what we shall become in the future. We only know that, if reality were to break through, we should reflect his likeness, for we should see him as he really is! Everyone who has at heart a hope like that keeps himself pure, for he knows how pure Christ is.

> I John 3:1-3
> J. B. Phillips' Translation
> New Testament in Modern English
> 1960 Edition

index

index

index